For all the
good girls

The Good Girl
Game Changers

First published by The Good Girl Game Changers, 2024.

Boonwurrung Country
PO Box 5135
Middle Park, VIC, 3206
Australia

The Good Girl Game Changers is located on Boonwurrung land and pays respect to the elders past and present, recognizing land was never ceded.

Text and illustrations copyright of The Good Girl Game Changers, 2024.

ISBN: 978-1-7638056-2-0

The moral right of the author/illustrator has been asserted.

All rights reserved. No parts of this publication may be reproduced without the publisher's prior permission.

The author has taken every reasonable precaution to verify the material in this book and assumes no liability for the content herein to the extent legally permissible.

Please note not every tool will be right for you. We encourage you to adjust your use of the information and recommendations accordingly. The author and the publisher assume no responsibility for your actions.

Illustrations: Lucia Benito

Design and Typesetting: Michelle Pirovich www.thesqueezebox.com.au

Editing: We acknowledge the use of Claude 3.5 Sonnet for proofreading and text enhancement in this book. The AI tool was used to check for grammar, spelling, and clarity. We confirm that we have personally reviewed and verified all AI-suggested edits to ensure accuracy and maintain the integrity of the work.

A Note on Gender:

 We acknowledge that 'girl' and 'woman' are socially constructed terms that cannot capture the beautiful complexity of human identity and expression. While our research focused on those groomed to be 'good girls,' we recognize that gendered expectations harm everyone—from boys pressured to be 'strong' to those whose identity exists beyond the binary.

The insights and tools in this journal emerged from women's experiences, but they speak to universal human needs for authenticity, belonging, and wellbeing. Regardless of how you identify, we welcome anyone who finds resonance in these pages.

The journey to break free from society's expectations and embrace our unique selves belongs to us all.

About the authors

We are two women who've lived the cost of society's 'good girl' rules and found our way to freedom. While our paths and perspectives differ, we share a commitment to helping others navigate this journey with evidence-based insights and practical tools.

Michelle (who goes by Chelle) is a globally recognized researcher, bestselling author, and wellbeing teacher who learned early that love was earned by performing perfectly, pleasing everyone, and protecting others. Despite excelling in her career, caring for her family, and collecting all the promised rewards, she found herself exhausted and empty. Through extensive research and personal healing, she uncovered how these beliefs contributed to patterns of abuse, poverty, and burnout in her life. Today, she combines scientific insights with lived experience to help women break free from society's 'good girl' expectations to live life on their own terms.

Evie is a former paramedic turned yoga teacher and somatic movement educator who uncovers another face of the 'good girl' narrative. After a decade of perfectionism led to burnout, she discovered that true strength comes not from suppressing her authentic self but from embracing it. Through therapy, yoga, and meditation, she learned to honor her body's subtle truths rather than ignore them. Now, she creates nurturing spaces where women can reconnect with their innate knowing and embrace their beautifully messy humanity.

As collaborators, we bring distinct voices to this work. Chelle is a feisty, white, queer, autistic, divorced, middle-aged mother of two boys who's learned to trust her own unique way of experiencing the world. Evie is a younger, grounded, nature-loving, white, straight, partnered woman who has found strength in embracing her sensitivity rather than hiding it. We acknowledge that our ability to "pass" in mainstream society comes with unearned privileges that have shaped our perspectives and opportunities. This awareness deepens our commitment to amplifying historically underrepresented voices and helping dismantle the oppressive beliefs we've both absorbed and continue to benefit from.

Most importantly, we recognize it is not our place to prescribe if, when, or how you might choose to challenge society's 'good girl' beliefs and behaviors. Your culture, relationships, experiences, and access to resources—particularly financial independence and local legislation—will shape what's right for you at any given moment. This journal is designed to support you in making more conscious choices about when to conform and when to resist based on your own circumstances, needs, and hopes.

Our deepest wish is that these pages offer you what we needed most on our own journeys: permission to be perfectly imperfect, tools to trust your inner wisdom and companions who understand both the cost and the courage of choosing to be uniquely you.

Contents

Section 1: In The Beginning...	**9**
Chapter 1: Learning To Be A 'Good Girl'	10
Chapter 2: Becoming 'Uniquely You'	15
Section 2: Getting Started...	**25**
Chapter 3: Using Your Journal	26
Chapter 4: Measuring Your Mindset	29
Section 3: Showing Self-Compassion...	**33**
Chapter 5: Self-Compassion Snapshot	34
Chapter 6: Self-Compassion – Feel It	39
Chapter 7: Self-Compassion – Release It	45
Chapter 8: Self-Compassion – Experiment With It	51
Chapter 9: Self-Compassion – Evolve It	57
Section 4: Securely Attaching	**63**
Chapter 10: Securely Attaching Snapshot	64
Chapter 11: Securely Attaching – Feel It	70
Chapter 12: Securely Attaching – Release It	76
Chapter 13: Securely Attaching – Experiment With It	82
Chapter 14: Securely Attaching – Evolve It	88

Section 5: Strengthening Self-Leadership	**95**
Chapter 15: Self-Leadership Snapshot	96
Chapter 16: Self-Leadership – Feel It	101
Chapter 17: Self-Leadership – Release It	107
Chapter 18: Self-Leadership – Experiment With It	113
Chapter 19: Self-Leadership – Evolve It	120
Additional Resources	**127**
Acknowledgements	**128**

Your journal is full of practical evidence-based exercises to help you break free of your 'good girl' beliefs and embody your unique self. If you'd like to download a PDF that contains all the exercises, please scan the code below.

Section 1 **In The Beginning...**

Chapter 1 **Learning To Be A 'Good Girl'**

Chelle's Story

I couldn't believe my luck. Having money left over from our weekly supermarket shop was rare. As the cashier counted the coins into my mother's hand, I waited with my fingers crossed.

Forty-two cents. "We have just enough," my mother said, turning to me. "You can pick one book."

I raced to the end of the checkout counter, my five-year-old heart pounding with possibility. There they stood: the Walt Disney Little Golden Books. As my eyes slowly scanned the beautiful book covers, I whispered my mother's words of caution: "Don't rush. Choose wisely."

Then I saw it—a bright yellow cover with hand-drawn illustrations of a little girl. In the center, she stood tall and serene, her hands folded over her stomach, looking straight into my eyes. But, around the cover edges, the same little girl appeared in a series of smaller poses. She poked out her tongue. She pulled her sister's hair. She threw a vase on the floor. She stuck her bottom in the air. She covered her face in shame. Having found myself in similar poses that morning, I grabbed the book with both hands.

"Good little, bad little girl," my mother read as I handed her the book. "Are you sure?"

I nodded eagerly. "I'm very sure."

You see, I knew those bad little girl poses all too well. Shouting, pouting, crying, and pulling my little sister's hair (it was long and blonde, and I hated it compared to my own dark locks) were how I handled the big feelings churning inside me. Each day seemed to end with my head buried in shame.

"Please be good," my mother would plead.

I tried. I really did. But it never lasted. Maybe this book held the secret to being the 'good girl' my mother wanted.

That night, tucked into our bunk beds, my sister and I listened as our mother began reading the book: "Once there was a good little girl and a bad little girl. They both lived together in the same house."

We learned that the good girl was neat as a pin; the bad girl was not. The good girl jumped from bed at Mummy's call; the bad girl hid under covers. The good girl waited quietly; the bad girl demanded attention. The good girl showed gratitude; the bad girl envied her sisters' things. The good girl ate slowly; the bad girl gobbled and asked for more.

As my mother read on, my stomach twisted into knots. I had done every one of those bad little girl behaviors—sometimes all in one day. With each word, the shame grew heavier: I was a bad little girl.

"Now, here's the big surprise," my mother read. "If you would be happy if you would be wise, open your ears and open your eyes. Make the bad little girl grow smaller and smaller. Make the good little girl grow taller and taller. And that is what she did. And when she was a good girl, she was a happy girl, and everyone was her friend. The end."

Wait! What? Could I be saved?

My mother set the book on our nightstand, kissed us goodnight, and turned off the light. But I lay awake in the dark, my young mind racing.

If I behaved more like the good little girl, could I make the bad little girl go away? Could all the fear, sadness, anger, and shame churning inside me disappear? Could I finally be happy and loved?

After hours of tossing and turning, I knew what I had to do. I would become a good little girl.

What happened next was not entirely my mother's fault. Each night at bedtime, I'd beg her to read the book again. She'd groan, open the cover, and begin. Soon, I'd memorized every one of those 'good girl' behaviors:

Be tidy.

Be obedient.

Be quiet.

Be patient.

Be selfless.

Be nice.

Be grateful.

And, for goodness sake, never eat too much.

In the weeks, months, years, and decades that followed, I attempted an impossible makeover. Piece by piece, I abandoned myself as I tried to become the 'good girl' others expected until I no longer recognized myself.

It wasn't entirely Walt Disney's fault. In 1978, despite the rising wave of feminism in Western cultures, our schools, churches, and communities relentlessly groomed us to be 'good girls.'

At school, polite obedience won us gold stars, but speaking out of turn brought swift punishment.

At church, dutiful sacrifice promised eternal salvation, but daring to put ourselves first guaranteed damnation.

In our families and communities, staying agreeable earned us love, while challenging unfairness made us outcasts.

The message followed us everywhere—through stories, songs, games, religion, laws, and social policies: only 'good girls' deserved safety and love.

It wasn't even entirely the fault of the men who were in power. Between 8000 and 3000 B.C., climate change and the rise of farming forced mass migrations, triggering violent tribal clashes. The winners created a new social order: they seized resources, killed men, and enslaved women and children. Their laws turned women into property through marriage, gave sons inheritance rights, and treated daughters as tradeable assets for alliances and profit. These ancient patterns—controlling women through marriage, money, and social status—laid the foundation for today's 'good girl' expectations.

I don't believe pointing fingers of blame solves anything. Across generations and cultures, we've created and sustained a system that grooms girls for compliance—teaching us to ignore our instincts, deny our needs, and stay silent in the face of abuse.

Some taught the 'good girl' story hoping to protect us; others used it to control us—either way, the damage has been devastating.

Our research with women worldwide exposes a brutal truth: this insidious grooming to be 'good girls'—agreeable, quiet, eager to please and care for others—warps our beliefs and behaviors and destroys lives. Beyond exhausting our spirits and shattering our sense of self, it leaves us vulnerable to sexual abuse, domestic violence, addiction, eating disorders, self-harm, burnout, and suicide.

I have lived this truth. My 'good girl' training ensured I kept the secrets of men who sexually abused me from ages four to fourteen, left me homeless by sixteen, and kept me trapped in abusive relationships as a young adult. It taught me early that safety came at the cost of silence.

By thirty-four, I had perfected the 'good girl' performance—collecting all the promised rewards: a loving family, a big career, financial security, good friends, a house full of nice things, and a passport full of stamps. Yet beneath this perfect facade, I was a stressed-out mess, grinding my teeth with the world's cruelest mantra: "Stupid. Useless. Selfish. You'll never be safe, happy, and loved if you don't try harder to be good."

No matter how hard I tried, it was never enough.

I was never enough. This was not how the story was meant to end.

Slowly, I began to retrace my steps. I went back to school and immersed myself in the science of human thriving, where I discovered that our brains are wired to be perfectly imperfect so we can learn, grow, and adapt. Through therapy, I learned that healthy relationships are equal, respectful, and mutual—allowing us to build genuine trust. Surrendering to spiritual curiosity helped me find peace within myself rather than trying to protect everyone else from life's pain.

Now, with grey hair and a body that aches and sags, I've found the courage, compassion, and care to be my unique self. I'm happily divorced, my children are leaving home, and I no longer care about my 'big' career. Most importantly, I've discovered what fitting in could never offer: the confidence to live life on my own terms while genuinely caring for others.

Before you dismiss this as just one old lady's tale that could never happen now, please look around. We've seen progress—Disney's first independent heroine in 'Frozen' (2013), Sweden's first gender-balanced cabinet (2014), and the #MeToo movement (2017). Yet the United Nations reports that women and girls in countries as diverse as Afghanistan and the United States now have fewer rights than their mothers and grandmothers did. Globally, women still face limited education and job prospects, restricted freedoms, and higher risks of poverty and violence. With women holding just 26.5% of worldwide parliamentary seats, it will take 286 years to secure legal protections against discrimination at our current pace. The 'good girl' story remains powerfully present.

Every adult has a responsibility to challenge these 'good girl' expectations that limit women's lives.

Instead, let's tell each other stories that celebrate our perfectly imperfect humanity. Let's nurture the curiosity, creativity, and courage that make each of us unique. Let's give ourselves and each other permission to learn and grow, even when it's messy and hard. Let's keep asking: "On whose terms and for whose benefit am I living my wild and precious life?"

It is our heartfelt hope this journal helps you find your own path to freedom.

Chapter 2 **Becoming 'Uniquely You'**

We're on a Zoom research call, watching memories flood our screen. Women from around the world—mostly cis white women aged 40-65 from the United States, Canada, the United Kingdom, Australia, and New Zealand—are sharing their earliest experiences of being taught to be 'good girls':

- I got a gold star from my teacher because I was being a 'good girl' who was quiet and still.
- After being naughty at school, I had to stand in the corner for not being a 'good girl.'
- I was told to "shush" at the dinner table because 'good girls' didn't have opinions they shared.
- When I was uncomfortable, sad, angry, or wanted to cry, my parents told me to be a 'good girl' and keep those feelings to myself.
- My Sunday School teacher explained that 'good girls' behaved well and didn't draw attention to themselves.
- My family told me that 'good girls' never made a fuss.
- My parents explained that 'good girls' should know that boys are more important. This was why I had to do housework and my brothers didn't.
- When I helped out around the house, my mother would tell me I was such a 'good girl.'
- My father told me to be a 'good girl' and look after my siblings to help my mother cope.
- My mother chastised me for digging loudly in the dirt with my brothers. She told me 'good girls' stayed clean and were quiet.
- I wasn't allowed to wear pants because 'good girls' dressed modestly.
- I heard people judging girls at school for wearing their skirts too short.

As we watch these stories fill our screens, our hearts break for the little girls we each were. Across the hundreds of stories shared, one very clear theme emerged: by the age of eleven, many of us had learned that *love is earned* by being the 'good girls' others expect.

To validate these patterns, we conducted a quantitative survey with more than 1,000 Australian women and found that 65% of the women felt pressured to be the 'good girl' others expected them to be. As a result, many of us have spent our lives twisting ourselves into emotional, physical, social, spiritual, and financial knots trying to:

- **Perform perfectly:** Fearing criticism, we chase an impossible ideal of effortless perfection in everything we do.
- **Please everyone:** Fearing rejection, we sacrifice our own wellbeing to meet others' endless expectations.
- **Protect others:** Fearing abandonment, we silence our truth to shield others from life's natural challenges.

Across all our data, the women tell us that these behaviors often win approval and love in the short term. But sustaining these behaviors leaves them exhausted, resentful, and disconnected from themselves. When they speak honestly, many share how these 'good girl' beliefs have contributed to their experiences of burnout, sexual abuse, domestic violence, poverty, addiction, eating disorders, self-harm, and thoughts of suicide.

Ours is not the first research to reveal these patterns.

Since the 1980s, Dr. Carol Gilligan and her colleagues at the Harvard Project on Women's Psychology and the Development of Girls have documented how girls around age eleven begin to lose connection with their authentic voices. Their research has found that girls who once spoke confidently about their thoughts and feelings begin to doubt and silence their true selves in response to cultural pressure to be 'good.' What starts as a conscious choice to maintain relationships gradually becomes an unconscious pattern of self-abandonment as girls learn to doubt their own knowing and silence their inner wisdom.

These patterns of silencing and self-abandonment cross cultural boundaries. For example, in the village of Titira in Ethiopia, the kidnapping of pre-pubescent girls for marriage remains an ancient and entrenched practice. Girls are lured from public places with promises of Coca-Cola or similar simple luxuries. The abductor and his male relatives then kidnap, circumcise, and rape the girl—acts considered physical markers of marriage that cannot be reversed.

Although abduction is illegal, the victims and their families remain silent. The circumcision makes it nearly impossible for the girl to marry anyone else. If reported to the police, village elders curse the family for disrupting community harmony and ostracizing them. No one will eat with them, work with them, touch them, or enter their home.

A 2014 study revealed that 63% of women surveyed in Titira reported at least one girl in their biological family had been abducted for marriage. How did this continue? No one ever talked about it. As one woman explained: "You can't have a word for something you don't say."

When researchers asked how several older girls had avoided abduction, they discovered their mothers had taught them to be assertive, confident, and critical thinkers. Neither naïve nor compliant, the demeanor of these girls deterred men who didn't want wives likely to cause problems. The men wanted 'good girls.'

Drawing inspiration from these Titiran mothers, we asked our research participants to share stories of resistance: What is the positive alternative to being a 'good girl'?

More slowly now, the women share their memories of those who defied society's 'good girl' expectations:

- Rebellious pop stars who refused to conform like Suzie Quatro and Madonna.
- Anne of Green Gables, the storybook character who stayed true to herself—often getting into trouble but always loved.
- My Grandma Bubbala typed 110 words a minute as an executive secretary in N.Y.C. and lived to 100.
- Me, when I spoke back to my mother.
- Watching Wonder Woman and Charlie's Angels on television and seeing women could be strong, capable, and independent.

- My aunt who was a disrespectful riot.
- A male teacher praised me for breaking a rule and showing initiative when a situation required flexibility.
- A college friend who was outspoken, dressed however she wanted, and lived by her own rules.
- Hillary Clinton who stood her ground against relentless criticism.
- Me, when I left my 'perfectly fine' marriage.

These stories of resistance fill our screens like beacons of hope, each showing a different path beyond 'good girl' expectations. When we ask the women what to call this alternative way of being, they debate: Is it being a 'brave girl'? A 'wise woman'? Should we reclaim what it means to be 'good'? Finally, they arrive at something simpler and more powerful: being 'uniquely you'—free from all gender expectations.

We validated these patterns once more with the Australian women, who confirmed that 38% *often* felt like the person they wanted to be, and 45% said they *sometimes* felt that way. The women tell us this freedom rests on the belief that *love is given* by:

- **Showing self-compassion:** Embracing our imperfections as the path to learning and growth.
- **Securely attaching:** Unapologetically prioritizing self-care and setting healthy boundaries in our relationships.
- **Strengthening Self-leadership:** Courageously speaking up and remaining true to ourselves.

Each of these factors is supported by decades of research on human thriving, offering evidence-based practices and tools for building these 'uniquely you' capabilities.

The women tell us that in the short term, these behaviors can come at the painful cost of the rejection, exclusion, and abandonment by others unhappy with our refusal to conform to their 'good girl' expectations. But like healthy food that nourishes, in the long-term, sustaining these behaviors leads to a greater sense of freedom, wellbeing, and belonging. As one woman explained: "It enables me to be accepted for who I am by others and also to accept myself."

Good Girl Beliefs

Perform Perfectly

Please Everyone

Protect Others

Junk Food Love

Uniquely You Mindset

Show Self-Compassion

Securely Attach

Strengthen Self-Leadership

Nutritious Love

These patterns of transformation from 'good girl' to 'uniquely you' echo across generations and cultures. Evie's own journey illustrates how the rewards of conformity can slowly poison our connection to self and how finding our way back to authenticity often requires completely reimagining what it means to be 'good.

Evie's Story

When I was four, my grandmother handed me a coveted Baby Born doll with a proud smile that reached her eyes.

"You've been doing as you're told, being a good girl," she said, placing the doll in my eager hands. Her words wrapped around me like a warm blanket, and in that moment, a mantra took root: *good girls get rewards*. This idea nestled in my young mind like a seed, sprouting tendrils that would eventually reach into every corner of my life—the reward for perfection, praise for keeping quiet, belonging for playing the expected part.

The pattern grew stronger with each passing year. In school, I excelled, never questioning authority, always being 'good.' My report cards were pristine monuments to compliance. Teachers called me "a pleasure to have in class"—code for a child who never caused trouble, never spoke out of turn, never challenged the status quo.

In my teens, I bleached my hair blonde and wore makeup that weighed down my eyelids, transforming myself into society's picture of acceptable femininity. Never mind that the bleach burned my scalp or that I hated those long hours trapped in the hairdresser's chair—looking a certain way felt like its own reward. Each compliment reinforced the lesson: changing myself to please others was the path to acceptance.

University brought new checklists of expectations, and I ticked every box with precision, hardly daring to ask myself, "What do I want?" That question felt dangerous, threatening to unravel the carefully constructed facade of the 'good girl' I'd become. Instead, I focused on what others wanted.

Then came the 'perfect' career—a highly esteemed role as a paramedic that fulfilled the checklist I'd written for myself so long ago. I was saving lives, respected, and achieving. I worked hard, took extra shifts, and never complained. On paper, it was everything I'd been groomed to want. But beneath the surface, something was dying.

I avoided anything that might crack my perfect exterior. I silenced my body's signals of exhaustion, ignored my heart's whispers for something different, and pushed away any hint of feeling inadequate or imperfect. I didn't know how to listen to myself anymore—there was no reward chart for authenticity, no gold star for speaking your truth.

But, like a house built on sand, it all collapsed. The burnout came not as a sudden storm but as a slow erosion of everything I thought I knew about myself. I quit my job, spiraling into a fog of exhaustion and confusion that no amount of 'being good' could fix. The rewards that had sustained me for so long turned to ashes in my mouth.

Therapy became my lifeline, where I finally met the woman I'd buried deep down—a girl who'd once known herself before the world taught her to perform instead of live. In that safe space, I began to reconnect with my wiser self, the one who knew how to simply be without needing a role or a reward.

I found my way to the yoga mat, seeking something quieter than achievement, something truer than perfection. In those still moments on the floor, with nothing to prove and no one to please, I simply was. I felt the years of tension unwind from my muscles and an ancient part of me stirring. I realized she had been there all along, waiting patiently for me to see her, to honor her, to finally understand that the greatest reward isn't in being good—it's in being real.

Today, I carry both versions of myself—the 'good girl' who learned to survive by pleasing others, and the unique woman who's learning to thrive by being herself. They're both part of my story, teaching me that true freedom comes not from performing perfectly but from having the courage to be perfectly imperfect.

Stories like Evie's and the experiences shared by our research participants align with Dr. Carol Gilligan's latest research in 'In A Human Voice.' Her work has evolved from seeing care ethics as a 'feminine' voice to recognizing how the gender binary itself—categorizing human capabilities as either 'masculine' or 'feminine'—serves as a cornerstone of patriarchal control. While conforming to expectations of 'real boys' and 'good girls' can win social acceptance and success, it requires disconnecting from our authentic selves. Men learn to hide their emotions; women learn to silence their needs. Either way, the cost is our humanity.

Healthy human development, Gilligan now argues, isn't about conforming to gendered expectations but about maintaining authentic relationships while speaking our truth. Her findings align with what our research participants discovered: we thrive when we can be both strong and vulnerable, independent and connected, caring for others while honoring our own needs. This is the path to being our unique selves.

The journey from 'good girl' to 'uniquely you' isn't a straight line but a continuum. Living in a world still governed by patriarchal expectations, there will be times when conforming keeps us safe or serves a purpose—just as we might occasionally choose convenient food over nutritious options. We must not judge ourselves or others for these choices. However, it's important to note that a steady diet of 'good girl' behaviors, like a diet of junk food, is likely to eventually leave us depleted and unwell.

Even in places like Titira, where women face severe restrictions, there are always small choices we can make toward authenticity. The mothers who taught their daughters to resist—to be assertive, confident, critical thinkers—show us what's possible. Each decision to be true to ourselves rather than conform is like choosing nourishing food over empty calories: it builds our strength, sustains our spirit, and keeps us well.

This journal is designed to help you pause and reflect: On whose terms and for whose benefit am I living my wild and precious life?

It's a choice each woman makes for herself, moment by moment, weighing safety against authenticity, conformity against truth. The insights and tools shared here are part of our evolving understanding of women's experiences. Use what resonates, adapt what doesn't, and share your discoveries. The work of undoing generations of 'good girl' conditioning cannot be done alone. But our collective consciousness, compassion, and courage may transform our world faster than we imagine.

Let's begin.

Section 2 **Getting Started...**

Chapter 3 **Using Your Journal**

There's no right way to use this journal—only your way. That's the beauty of a perfectly imperfect journey. You can't get this wrong.

To make the most of your energy and time, this tip for our research can help: while it's tempting to start by tackling 'good girl' behaviors head-on, we've discovered that focusing on developing our strengths creates faster, more sustainable change. When we invest in building capabilities that help us thrive, our confidence grows stronger, our relationships become more authentic, our creativity flows more freely, and our wellbeing deepens. Research shows this strengths-based approach can accelerate our growth up to three times faster than focusing on what we want to change. Plus, it gives us more energy for life instead of exhausting ourselves with self-criticism and correction.

Building on our research with women worldwide, the following pages offer evidence-based practices for building on the 'uniquely you' factors for:

- **Showing self-compassion:** Embracing our imperfections as the path to learning and growth.
- **Securely attaching:** Unapologetically prioritizing self-care and setting healthy boundaries in our relationships.
- **Strengthening Self-leadership:** Courageously speaking up and remaining true to ourselves.

Each factor draws on decades of human thriving research, offering practical tools to build these capabilities. To help you explore these insights with ease and joy, we've created our FREE framework:

FREE framework

Feel it

Release it

Experiment with it

Evolve it

- **Feel it:** Uncover what your emotions tell you about why this matters.
- **Release it:** Move your body to process or celebrate these feelings.
- **Experiment with it:** Get curious about what research suggests, and your intuition knows.
- **Evolve it:** Welcome the learning opportunities in each step forward.

You'll find a variety of gentle invitations: guided meditations, journaling exercises, somatic practices, cognitive challenges, and emotional releases. Each one is designed to help you break free from 'good girl' beliefs and embody your unique self.

How do you choose what's right for you?

You're welcome to follow your intuition, flipping through to find pages that call to you. Or, if you prefer more structure:

- **Measure your mindset:** Test which 'good girl' beliefs and behaviors might be holding you back.
- **Follow your energy:** Choose the 'uniquely you' factor you want to build—not should build, but truly want to develop right now.
- **Accelerate your learning:** Discover how your chosen factor helps break free from 'good girl' patterns.
- **Play with FREE tools:** Select practices that resonate with your current situation and goals.

Remember: this isn't a race to some finish line. There are no gold stars to earn. Ambition and performance—those familiar 'good girl' habits—won't serve you here. Instead, choose a pace of grace that feels right for you.

You can set this journal aside and return to it whenever you're ready. For many of us, this is lifetime work. Know that you're in good company.

If you need support beyond what these pages can offer, reach out to us at **www.thegoodgirlgamechangers.com**.

If working with these tools stirs up overwhelming feelings, please connect with a trained therapist or coach. You'll find our recommended resources listed on our website.

Chapter 4 **Measuring Your Mindset**

After exploring how 'good girl' expectations shape our lives and discovering what it means to be 'uniquely you,' you might be wondering: Where do I stand right now? How deeply have these patterns affected me?

You can take the Good Girl Mindset Survey online for free at **www.thegoodgirlgamechangers.com** or by scanning the QR code and immediately receive your scores.

Or use the questions below and on the following page.

Over the past two weeks, how often have you found yourself caught between society's expectations and your authentic self? Take a moment to reflect on each statement below, scoring from 0 (never) to 10 (always):

Performing Perfectly

Remember how we learned that by age eleven, many of us believe we must earn love through perfect performance? Let's explore how this shows up in your life:

	Score
To avoid criticism, I tried hard to be perfect.	
I was disapproving and judgmental about my own flaws and inadequacies.	
When I was struggling, I tended to separate and cut myself off from others.	
When I experienced problems, I was consumed by feelings of anxiety and worry.	
Self-Compassion Score (add the four items above)	

Pleasing Everyone

Think about those moments when keeping connections meant losing yourself:

	Score
To avoid rejection, I prioritized pleasing others before taking care of myself.	
I struggled to set healthy boundaries to prioritize my self-care.	
I found it hard to trust other people.	
I was resentful about the sacrifices I made for others.	
Secure Attachment Score (add the four items above)	

Protecting Others

Consider how often you silence your truth to keep others comfortable:

	Score
To avoid being abandoned, I protected others by silencing my true feelings.	
I was scared to speak up for myself or others.	
I did not feel there was real purpose in my life.	
I was not the person I wanted to be.	
Protecting Others Score (add the four items above)	

Understanding Your Results

Your scores reveal both the strength of 'good girl' patterns and your 'uniquely you' capabilities. Think of them as two ends of a continuum—the lower your 'good girl' score, the more you're already embracing your authentic self; the higher your score, the more these old 'good girl' beliefs might be holding you back.

More important than any one number is how you feel about your scores and what actions you want to take next. For example:

- **Scores 0-12**: You've already built strong 'uniquely you' capabilities. Low scores in *Performing Perfectly* suggest strong self-compassion skills. Low scores in *Pleasing Everyone* suggest secure attachment skills. Low scores in *Protecting Others* suggest strong Self-leadership skills.
- **Scores 13-31**: You're in transition, balancing between old 'good girl' patterns and authentic expression. Notice which areas feel most challenging. Celebrate where you're already breaking free.
- **Scores 32-40**: Your 'good girl' beliefs may be limiting your freedom. These patterns once helped you survive, but if they leave you feeling exhausted, overwhelmed, or lost, you can now choose different ways to thrive.

Choosing Your Path Forward

Look at your scores across the three 'uniquely you' factors. Which section calls to you most strongly? Where do you feel most ready for change? Remember—this isn't about fixing what's 'wrong.' It's about choosing where to invest your energy next:

- If perfect performance exhausts you, explore the Self-Compassion section.
- If people-pleasing leaves you resentful, dive into Secure Attachment.
- If protecting others silences your truth, start with Self-Leadership.

Or simply trust your intuition and choose the capability that feels most important for you right now. That's where your energy wants to flow.

Remember: These scores aren't judgments about who you are or what you're capable of—they're invitations to explore how you want to navigate this world. They help you choose which tools in the following chapters might serve you best as you build your unique way of being.

This isn't about getting it 'right.' It's about understanding yourself better so you can answer that crucial question: "On whose terms and for whose benefit am I living my wild and precious life?"

Please note your survey results and the tools provided are not intended to replace personal psychological support. If any of our materials leave you feeling upset or distressed, please reach out to a trained therapist.

Section 3 **Showing Self-Compassion...**

Chapter 5 **Self-Compassion Snapshot**

Our research with women worldwide revealed how perfectionism emerges as a survival strategy to win safety and love. Women reported intense pressure to achieve flawlessly across all areas of life, with more than 77% admitting they strived for perfection to avoid criticism. "To avoid criticism, I tried hard to be perfect," shared one woman, while another explained, "Being perfect was required to be accepted and valued." For many, this wasn't just about meeting personal goals—it was deeply tied to societal expectations that women must perform perfectly, please constantly, and maintain a flawless facade to prove their worth.

The toll of this relentless pursuit is devastating, with over 82% of women reporting exhaustion and burnout from maintaining impossible standards. "I was renowned for my generosity and would give and give and give to my own detriment," one woman confessed, while another shared, "I worked harder and harder to perform well in the hope that I could prove myself worthy." This perfectionism leaves little room for self-care or compassion, trapping women in cycles of overwork and self-neglect just to maintain the appearance of having it all together. The findings make clear that perfectionism isn't merely a personal struggle but a systemic issue with profound consequences for women's wellbeing.

Dr. Kristin Neff's research reveals why perfectionism has such a powerful grip on women's lives. Our brains are wired to ensure our survival by scanning for threats and keeping us safe within our social groups. But when we're groomed to believe our imperfections make us unworthy of love and belonging, this survival system turns against us. We begin to see ourselves as the threat—attacking with self-criticism ("I'm such an idiot"), isolating ourselves in shame ("I can't do anything right"), and ruminating over our perceived failures ("I'll never be good enough"). What starts as an attempt to protect ourselves becomes a prison of perfectionism that leaves us feeling more vulnerable and alone than ever.

Self-compassion offers a different path. Instead of exhausting ourselves fighting against our imperfections, Dr. Neff's research shows we can learn to meet our struggles with understanding and care. This begins with recognizing that our inner critic, though harsh, is actually trying to keep us safe—it's just going about it in a way that leaves us feeling more vulnerable and alone.

Dr. Neff's research has found that women particularly benefit from two complementary forms of self-compassion working in balance:

- **'Tender self-compassion'** provides the safe haven we need when we're struggling—the gentle voice that says, "This is really hard," and the soothing presence that helps us feel worthy of care even when we're falling short of perfection.
- **'Fierce self-compassion'** provides the protective force we need to create meaningful change—the powerful voice that says, "This isn't okay," and the courageous energy that helps us stand up for ourselves, set healthy boundaries, and challenge the societal expectations that leave us hustling for perfection. Like the assertive mothers in Titira who taught their daughters to resist harmful cultural practices, fierce self-compassion helps us protect and fight for ourselves with the same strength we'd use to protect someone we love.

It's this combination of nurturing and strength that makes self-compassion such a powerful force for change. Yet the most persistent myth about self-compassion is that it makes us soft. Studies consistently show the opposite: when we practice self-compassion, we become more likely to acknowledge our mistakes, learn from failures, and maintain high standards. The difference is that we do this from a place of growth and possibility rather than fear and shame.

By activating our brain's caregiving and self-awareness systems, self-compassion helps us challenge the message most girls absorb by age eleven—that they must earn love by performing perfectly. Rather than undermining our motivation, this helps us trust our capabilities, maintain our standards, and build our resilience—all while treating ourselves with the same wisdom and kindness we'd offer a good friend.

This may explain why self-compassion emerged as the most powerful tool in our research for breaking free from 'good girl' perfectionism. It creates space for us to be authentically human, neither perfect nor flawed, but genuinely ourselves. "It enables me to accept that I'm learning just like everyone else," one woman shared. "Instead of beating myself up when I fall short, I can be kind to myself and keep growing."

Michelle Obama's journey offers a powerful example of this transformation from perfectionism to self-compassion. In her memoir "Becoming," she describes her early life being driven by what she calls a "checklist mentality"—constantly striving to be "the perfect Black woman" by getting the best grades, attending top schools (Princeton, Harvard Law), and landing prestigious jobs. "I have been trained, as so many of us are," she reflects, "to push through pain, push through discomfort, push through bad experiences."

But like many women in our research, she eventually discovered that this relentless perfectionism was unsustainable. During her time as First Lady—a role that came with intense scrutiny and impossible expectations—she began practicing what she calls "self-compassionate truth-telling." Where she once berated herself with thoughts like "I'm not doing enough" or "I should be handling this better," she learned to speak to herself with understanding: "Hey, you're doing the best you can right now" and "You don't have to be Superwoman. Perfection isn't the goal—being present and authentic is."

In her podcast conversations, she shares how she reframes moments of self-doubt: "Instead of thinking 'I'm failing because I'm struggling,' I now tell myself 'I'm human, and humans struggle sometimes.'" She particularly emphasizes this gentler self-talk when dealing with body image and aging: "Rather than criticizing my body for changing, I thank it for carrying me through life and tell myself, 'You're exactly where you need to be right now.'"

Her story echoes what our research consistently shows: the path beyond perfectionism isn't about lowering our standards but about changing how we relate to ourselves when we inevitably fall short of impossible ideals. It's about finding the courage to be both ambitious and human, to pursue excellence while treating ourselves with the same understanding we'd offer a good friend.

In this section of your journal, you'll find evidence-based practices designed to help you build these essential self-compassion capabilities. Using our F.R.E.E framework introduced in Chapter 3, these tools will help you:

- **Feel It:** Learn to recognize when your inner critic is activated and name the emotions and fears driving your need for perfection. Tools like 'Name the Pain' will help you identify what your perfectionism is trying to protect you from.
- **Release It:** Use breathwork, movement, and touch to calm your nervous system when perfectionism has you in its grip. Practices like 'Breathe in Love' and 'Grab An Oxytocin Shot' will help you find safety in your body.
- **Experiment with It:** Try new ways of relating to yourself with kindness rather than criticism. Tools like 'Be a YETI' (You're not there... Yet!) will help you embrace the messy magic of learning.
- **Evolve It:** Transform your relationship with imperfection through self-compassionate reflection. Practices like 'Run A Learning Loop' will help you grow from challenges without shame.

You can work through these tools step-by-step or choose the practice that most calls to you at any moment. Remember, this isn't about performing self-compassion perfectly—it's about finding gentle ways to free yourself from perfectionism's grip and embrace your perfectly imperfect humanity.

Just as the journey from 'good girl' to 'uniquely you' exists on a continuum, building self-compassion is a practice, not a destination. There will be times when your inner critic feels overwhelming and times when kindness flows naturally. What matters is not doing it perfectly but staying curious about what you need in each moment to feel safe, supported, and true to who you are.

FEEL IT

Release Discomfort
Soothe your nervous system by breathing in and being honest about the pain you're feeling, and then releasing it as you roar the breath out.

Shuffle The Story
If you're overwhelmed by negative thoughts ask: "Is this story true? What other explanations might I have missed about this situation?"

Name The Pain
Ask yourself: "How am I feeling?" When you're ready answer: "I feel …" Don't dismiss the emotions, try to listen without judgment.

RELEASE IT

Grab An Oxytocin Shot
Place one hand over the opposite wrist and breathe deeply for at least 7 breaths to lower your cortisol (stress) and induce oxytocin (calm).

Be Soothed By Nature
Head to a favorite spot in nature, sit quietly, and breathe mindfully as you appreciate the wonders of the world around you.

Breathe In Love
As you breath in say "I am safe" as you breathe out say "I am, loved". Repeat trying to make your breath a little deeper each time.

EXPERIMENT WITH IT

Be A Yeti
Rather than letting your inner critic run wild, when you're struggling remind yourself: "I'm not there yet. I just need more time, effort, or practice."

Best Friend Letter
What might a best friend say to you? How might they encourage you to take accountability? What small step might they suggest?

Set A Learning Goal
Set a tiny learning goal that can have a mighty impact towards the outcomes you want to achieve. Don't be afraid to ask for help.

EVOLVE IT

Tap It Out
Release the messiness of learning by tapping key meridian points on your body as you help your brain turn challenges into opportunities.

Take A Victory Lap
Savor and celebrate the effort you are making and the learning you are gaining. You have every reason to feel proud of your choices.

Run A Learning Loop
Grab your journal and ask: What went well? Where did I struggle? What did I learn? What can I try next? Note down your insights.

Chapter 6 **Self-Compassion – Feel It**

the SOONER we feel it
the FASTER we heal it

Addiction

Chelle's Story

I'm ten years old, the back of my bare legs sticking to a hard plastic chair in our stuffy school gymnasium. The air is thick with end-of-year restlessness, floor polish, and the stale smell of fidgeting children. I'm already dreaming of escape when the principal announces the Student of the Year award. My mind drifts—I'm not the kind of girl who wins things.

I'm never the 'good' girl they want. Where 'good girls' stay quiet, I burst with words. Where 'good girls' act considerate, I blurt out the wrong thing at the wrong time. Where 'good girls' follow the rules, I break them. No matter how I try to fold myself into that 'good girl' mold, I never quite fit.

So when the principal calls my name, the sound feels foreign in my ears. As I peel my legs off the chair, the gymnasium erupts into applause. As I cross that stage, for the first time in my life, I see what I've been missing in all those faces: Admiration. Respect. Belonging.

After the ceremony, my mother wraps me in a crushing hug, whispering words I've never heard from her before: "I'm so proud of you." In that moment, a dangerous idea takes root: perfect performance equals love. Here, finally, is my path to becoming the 'good girl' everyone expects.

The addiction grows quietly at first, then faster. Each achievement becomes a fix: perfect grades, prestigious jobs, endless volunteering. I climb the corporate ladder with the same desperate determination that once earned me that plastic trophy. At home, I exhaust myself being the ideal wife, mother, daughter, and friend—treating praise like oxygen. Bosses praise my tireless work ethic; family celebrates my endless caregiving; friends speak of me with awe.

Like any addiction, the more I feed it, the more it hollows me out. But I can't stop. Over-functioning becomes my protection against anything real or raw. Each time anxiety or self-doubt creeps in, I frantically reach for the next fix: another project, another event, another committee, anything I can tick off for that dopamine hit.

Other people's admiration is the perfect drug. It looks clean. Respectable. Professional. But like any drug, it's never enough. Each hit of validation leaves me craving more, desperate to maintain the high of being "good enough," terrified of the crash that comes with falling short.

Recovery only starts when I finally see the truth: no amount of performing perfectly can fill the void that only self-acceptance can heal. Because real love—the kind that sets us free—never demands a performance. It simply invites us to show up exactly as we are. Messy. Imperfect. And absolutely worthy.

RELEASE DISCOMFORT
Showing Self-Compassion: Feel It

If you're beating yourself up with criticism, self-judgment, or shame, take a few minutes to soothe your nervous system by using a lion's breath to release these painful feelings from your body.

1. **Find a comfortable seated position:** You can sit on a chair or the floor, whichever feels the most comfortable for you. Place your hands over your knees and spread your fingers wide. Let your shoulders drop down. Relax your jaw. Close your eyes.

2. **Breathe into what hurts:** Take a slow, deep breath in through your nose. As you're inhaling, let yourself feel whatever uncomfortable emotions you are struggling with right now. Don't try to dismiss the feelings, fight them, or fix them. Just let yourself feel them fully, knowing it will be just for the length of your breath.

3. **Breathe out strongly and roar the hurt out:** When you're ready, imagine you can see the uncomfortable feelings being pushed out from your body as you exhale strongly. Do this by opening your mouth wide, and as you stick out your tongue and stretch it down towards your chin, push the air from your belly as you make the sound "ha." If it helps, pretend you are a lion roaring.

4. **Breathe normally (and laugh):** Take a few normal breaths. Laugh at how ridiculous and/or relieved you feel if desired.

5. **Repeat your roaring breath:** Repeat steps 2, 3, and 4 as needed until your nervous system feels calmer.

Inspired by: Tina Bruce

NAME THE PAIN
Showing Self-Compassion: Feel It

Rather than ignoring, numbing, or protecting yourself against emotional pain, mindfully turn toward the discomfort and acknowledge how you're feeling. Don't dismiss the feeling; just try to listen without judgment.

1. **Find a quiet and safe place:** Sit and take a few slow breaths. If you like to journal, you may find it helpful to have a pen and paper handy.

2. **Ask yourself, "How am I feeling?":** Don't rush for an answer. Sit with the question as you slowly let it breathe through your body.

3. **When you're ready to answer, "I feel …":** Try to avoid using "I am …" to describe how you're feeling. Your feelings don't define who you are. They're just a momentary reaction to what you're experiencing.

If you're struggling to identify what you're feeling, use the list below.

😞 SAD	😠 MAD	😣 HURT	😨 SCARED
○ Disappointed	○ Annoyed	○ Shocked	○ Worried
○ Disillusioned	○ Offended	○ Criticized	○ Anxious
○ Vulnerable	○ Frustrated	○ Jealous	○ Insecure
○ Guilty	○ Angry	○ Rejected	○ Threatened
○ Lonely	○ Bitter	○ Humiliated	○ Ashamed
○ Depressed	○ Betrayed	○ Victimized	○ Abandoned

4. **Follow up with, "What else do I need to know …":** Uncomfortable feelings are your body's way of getting your attention. If you feel safe to continue, ask what triggered the feeling/s, how is it impacting you, and why does it matter to you?

Inspired by: Susan David

SHUFFLE THE STORY

Showing Self-Compassion: Feel It

If you're overwhelmed by negative thoughts and self-criticism, try asking yourself, *"Is this story true? What other explanations might I have missed about this situation?"* This isn't about denying reality or forcing positivity—it's about recognizing that our initial interpretations are often shaped by our fears and past hurts rather than the full picture of what's happening. For example:

Old Story	Shuffled Story
I'm not good enough	I'm learning & growing
I should be farther along	I'm where I'm meant to be
I'm too much for people	I am enough
I let others down	I try my best for others

Over time, these practices can help to rewire your brain, shifting old thought patterns toward more supportive, balanced perspectives. Below is a space for you to reshuffle the stories of self-criticism that no longer serve you well:

Old Story	Shuffled Story

Inspired by: Carol Dweck

Chapter 7 **Self-Compassion – Release It**

> You are Perfectly imperfect just like EVERYONE ELSE

Too Much
Evie's Story

I'm five years old, pressed against my father's leg at another family party, while laughter and chatter swirl around us like storm clouds. Every unfamiliar face that looms close sends fresh tears streaming down my cheeks. My body feels too big, too small, too everything at once in this space I don't know how to navigate. The adults roll their eyes over my head, their whispers carrying that familiar word—delivered like a doctor's diagnosis: "emotional."

"Dad, I want to go home." I'd whine.

The adults would laugh—those light, sparkly party laughs. I'd grip my dad's leg tighter while they joked in conversation with my dad, "Oh, you've got a little cling-on."

My dad, bless him, crouches down to my level, "It's okay to cry, Bean. Sometimes I cry too."

And for a while, I believed him. For a while, the shame would quiet when he whispered those words.

But then the world started teaching me otherwise.

In 2007, I watched the world crucify Britney Spears for having the audacity to break down in public. Every tabloid screamed "unstable," "crazy," "too emotional"—as if her pain was a personal failing rather than a human response to impossible demands.

I was twelve, watching, learning: this is what happens to women who let their emotions out. The shame I'd felt as a little girl now had headlines to prove it was justified.

The lesson continued through relationships:

"Don't cry."

"Why are you being so sensitive?"

"You're too emotional."

Each comment another reason to dam up my feelings. I made myself smaller and smaller, more contained, and more controlled. I thought if I could just be less—less emotional, less sensitive—I would finally be enough. The irony of that math still astounds me.

Here's what I've learned since then: Crying is my body's way of processing, of cleansing, of speaking truths too big for words.

These days, I can regulate the flow better—I'm not that overwhelmed little girl anymore—but I'm no longer ashamed when tears come.

I'm done trying to be less to make others more comfortable. Those tears they called "too emotional"? They're actually just right. They're mine. They're me. And I'd rather be too much than not enough of myself.

GRAB AN OXYTOCIN SHOT
Showing Self-compassion: Release It

Quickly ease your feelings of anxiety and stress (cortisol hormones) and increase your sense of peace (oxytocin hormones) by gently placing your hands on your body in a way that feels comforting and reassuring. Try to tune into how your body responds to find the approach that suits you best.

1. **Place one hand over the opposite wrist:** You can do this seated with your hands resting on your lap or placed on top of a table. You can also do this standing with your arms crossed in front of you or clasped behind your back.

2. **Take three slow, deep breaths:** As you hold your wrist gently and reassuringly, try to slow and deepen your breath. You want to stay in this position as you breathe in and out for at least six seconds to help release your oxytocin hormones and calm your nervous system.

3. **Notice how your body is feeling:** Is your jaw softening? Are your shoulders relaxing? Does your body feel calmer? Continue holding your wrist and slowing breathing as needed until you feel your body has released the feelings of anxiety and stress.

Inspired by: Jane McGonigal

BREATHE IN LOVE
Showing Self-Compassion: Release It

If you're struggling to embrace your imperfections, place your hands on your body warmly and speak soothing words to reassure yourself that you're safe. The safer you feel, the more curious, creative, and caring you can be with yourself and others.

1. **Soften your body:** Sit somewhere comfortable and quiet. Place one hand on top of the other and cover your heart. Close your eyes or soften your gaze down towards the floor. As you take a slow breath in, relax your jaw. As you take a slow breath out, let your shoulders drop down. Repeat this step for three breaths, letting your heart and body soften a little further each time.

2. **Soothe your mind:** As you take your next slow breath in, say to yourself: "I am safe." As you take your next slow breath out, say to yourself: "I am loved." Repeat this step for five breaths, letting each reminder soothe and reassure your heart and mind.

3. **Embrace your imperfection:** Continue to sit quietly with your hands resting over your heart and breathing gently. Remind yourself that you are perfectly imperfect, just like everyone else. No one has it all figured out. Like you, they're just doing the best they can with what they have each day and learning from what unfolds. Ask yourself: "What is the wisest and kindest thing my imperfect heart can learn from what's unfolding right now?" Let your body answer as honestly as you can.

Inspired by: Kristin Neff

BE SOOTHED BY NATURE

Showing Self-Compassion: Release It

When you're feeling overwhelmed by perfectionism or self-criticism, nature can help regulate your nervous system and restore your sense of peace. Even brief encounters

1. Choose your connection: You don't need perfect conditions or lots of time; even a few minutes with nature can help reduce your stress hormones and increase your feelings of wellbeing. Try:

SKY GAZING	WATER WATCHING	TREE TIME	GARDEN GROUNDING	ANIMAL APPRECIATION
Watch the clouds drift or stars twinkle.	Listen to the soothing sound of water.	Be still under a tree and breath in its strength.	Bury your bare hands or feet in healthy soil.	Notice animals moving wild and free.

2. Engage your senses: As you connect with your chosen element of nature. What do you see? What do you hear? What do you feel? What do you smell? What do you sense?

3. Follow nature's rhythm: Let nature's pace guide you. Breathe slowly and deeply. Notice nature's unhurried timing. Observe how nothing in nature strives for perfection. Allow yourself to simply be, just as nature does.

4. Carry it forward: Like nature, you don't need to rush. Like nature, you can flow with change. Like nature, you are perfectly imperfect. Like nature, you belong exactly as you are.

Inspired by: Barbara Fredrickson

Chapter 8 **Self-Compassion – Experiment With It**

Limitations

Chelle's Story

I started small, with the kinds of lies 'good girls' tell to stay safe: blaming my sister for the broken vase, pocketing coins from mother's purse. As I grew up, my lies became an armor of deceptions that felt necessary for survival: padding my resume with embellished achievements, denying a mean comment about a colleague, inventing excuses to avoid helping friends move, refusing to take ownership for the fart that made everyone gag. Each lie was another way to hide my imperfections, to maintain the illusion of being 'good.'

But the hardest lies were the ones I told myself. That I was fine. That I was handling everything. That if I just tried harder, worked longer, did better, I'd finally be worthy of love.

Behind my shield of perfectionism, I waged a relentless war against myself. My inner critic never rested: "You're such a fraud." "You're lazy." "You're worthless." I believed if I just criticized myself enough, shamed myself enough, hated myself enough, I would finally become a perfect person who deserved to be loved.

Then came the Halloween candy incident. I'd eaten the last of my son's trick-or-treat stash, then when he discovered the missing chocolate blamed his Dad for throwing it out. As I sat in therapy beating myself up over my lies, my therapist asked: "How would you respond if your son had done that?"

I sat there, stunned. The harsh words I'd been using against myself suddenly felt like poison in my mouth. Because I knew exactly how I'd respond to my son. I wouldn't shame him or deny him love until he earned it back. But—and this was crucial—I also wouldn't brush it off or pretend it didn't matter.

Instead, I'd sit with him in that uncomfortable space where we face our mistakes honestly. I'd ask what was happening in his heart when he made that choice. I'd acknowledge the hurt his actions caused while believing in his capacity to do better. I'd help him take responsibility—to apologize, to make amends, to learn from what happened. I'd support him in figuring out what this moment taught him about who he wants to be and what he needs to do differently next time.

I'd be the wise and kind friend who holds him accountable while never doubting his worth.

Because real growth doesn't happen through self-punishment or self-protection—it happens through self-compassion. We don't learn by beating ourselves up or hiding from our truth. We grow by facing ourselves honestly, by treating our mistakes not as evidence of our unworthiness but as opportunities to improve.

These days, when I bump up against my limitations, fall short of my ideals, and sometimes flat-out fail (and I still do, because I'm human), I try to meet myself with the same wisdom and kindness I'd offer my son. To ask myself: What was happening for me in that moment? What do I need to own? How do I want to learn and grow?

The hard truth is that self-compassion requires more courage than self-criticism ever did. It means standing in that uncomfortable space between who we are and who we want to be, without hiding or attacking ourselves. It means learning to be both honest and kind with ourselves, especially in those moments when we least want to be.

And yes, sometimes I still eat my kid's Halloween candy. But now I own it, apologize, and use it as another chance to practice being the wise and kind friend I'm learning to be—not just for my son, but finally, for myself.

BE A YETI

Showing Self-Compassion: Experiment With It

If you're bumping up against your limitations, making mistakes, or falling short of your ideals, you are not a failure. You're just "not yet" where you want to be. The good news is that your talents, intelligence, and abilities can continue with further effort, practice, support, and learning.

1. **Listen carefully:** When you're struggling, what do you say to yourself in these moments? Do you beat yourself up and point out what a disappointment you are? Do you pump yourself up and rob yourself of important feedback? Or are you honest with yourself about your strengths and struggles?

2. **Be a YETI:** Give yourself the permission and support you need to keep learning by reminding yourself that you always have the potential for growth. For example:

I haven't learned	... YET
I haven't figured it out	... YET
I'm not good at this	... YET
I don't understand	... YET
I can't	... YET
I haven't mastered	... YET

3. **Ask for help:** Who can help you figure out your next YETI step? Who could share their experiences? Where could you learn these skills? Might a coach or mentor help? Can you find an accountability buddy?

Inspired by: Carol Dweck

SET A LEARNING GOAL

Showing Self-Compassion: Experiment With It

Embrace your imperfections by turning the outcomes you want into tiny learning goals that spark your curiosity and give you the confidence to shamelessly ask for help, try new approaches, and seek feedback as you grow.

1. **Spark your curiosity:** Flex your brain muscles by choosing a tiny learning goal that can have a mighty impact. You can fill in the blanks below to help you figure it out:

    The outcome I want is _____.

    It's important to me because _____.

    While I can't control _____,

    I can get curious about _____.

    This would help me to learn _____.

    and be useful because _____.

    Based on this, the tiny but mighty learning goal I want to set is
    _____.

    Success looks like _____.

2. **Experiment:** Act on your learning goal within the next 24–48 hours. Can you ask someone for help? Is there a new skill you can practice or an existing skill you can build upon? Remember, as long as you show up, give your goal your best shot, and stay curious about the results, you can't fail.

3. **Tune into feedback:** Measure your progress. Ask other people for their feedback. Reflect on what you're learning. How can you use this growth to move you closer to the outcomes you most want?

Inspired by: Carol Dweck

BEST FRIEND LETTER
Showing Self-Compassion: Experiment With It

By writing to ourselves like we're writing to a dear friend, we can bypass our inner critic and access the wisdom and compassion we already possess. This shift in perspective makes it easier to respond to our struggles with curiosity rather than judgment. Use the W.R.I.T.E framework below to guide you:

1. **Welcome the feelings:** Start with "Dear [your name]," and acknowledge what you're struggling with right now. Be specific about the emotions and thoughts coming up.

2. **Remember your humanity:** Remind yourself that everyone faces similar challenges. For example: *"Making mistakes in relationships is part of being human. You're not alone in this perfectly imperfect experience."*

3. **Imagine the support:** Write what your wisest, most caring friend would say to you. What understanding would they offer? What perspective might they share?

4. **Trust your strength:** Highlight your capabilities and past experiences. For example: *"Remember last year's difficult project? You felt overwhelmed but broke it down into smaller steps, asked for help, and found your way through. You have that same strength now."*

5. **Express encouragement:** Close with specific words of support. What do you most need to hear right now? Be sure to Sign the letter: *"With love and understanding, [your name]"*

Inspired by: Kristin Neff

Chapter 9 **Self-Compassion – Evolve It**

Pilgrimage
Chelle's Story

I stand in a Portuguese town square, staring at my phone's useless maps, the weight of my barely-familiar backpack cutting into my shoulders. The yellow arrows that should mark my path have vanished, and my carefully planned pilgrimage unravels on day one. My inner voice has a field day: "This is what happens when you attempt things you're not prepared for."

Just months from turning fifty, I've chosen to walk 120 kilometers alone through Portugal and Spain on the Camino Portugues. This isn't like me. I'm the woman who only attempts things I can excel at. In meetings, I speak only when certain. In relationships, I carefully script conversations. My life is a masterclass in controlled success.

But something about this pilgrimage whispers to my soul. For a decade, I've collected others' Camino stories, each one stirring something wild and wanting inside me. Now, instead of letting my limitations become permanent barriers, I try something different. I look at each fear and add one tiny word: "yet."

I haven't hiked this far... yet.

I haven't navigated foreign countries alone... yet.

I haven't spent nine days in my own company... yet.

That tiny word becomes my compass. Each "yet" transforms into action: buying a good backpack, taking weekend hiking trips with friends, learning basic Spanish, strengthening my legs.

The night before departure, my stomach twists in knots. I sit on my bed, surrounded by hiking gear I barely know how to use, my inner good girl questioning every decision that has led me here. But I keep reminding myself: I'm not failing at this journey. I just haven't started it... yet.

Day one delivers my lesson in humility. A simple six-kilometer walk becomes a three-hour adventure as I lose the trail markers and circle an entire Portuguese town. By day two, my heels are raw with blisters, and I mime "bandaid" in a pharmacy. But something beautiful emerges: local villagers call out "Buen Camino!" as I stumble past—not just wishing me "happy trails" but offering their support as I wind my way along this unpredictable journey.

As the days unfold, everything shifts. Wrong turns reveal unexpected views across misty valleys. Awkward conversations with strangers transform into bridges of connection. Even the blisters offer lessons about healing while moving forward. Each morning, instead of obsessing about the remaining kilometers, I ask only: "What's the next right step?"

Sometimes, this means walking slower than planned. Sometimes, it means taking alternative paths. Always, it means releasing my 'good girl' need for perfection.

Nine days later, I sink onto the cobblestones in front of Santiago de Compostela's cathedral, and something inside me breaks open. Tears stream down my face—not just from physical exhaustion but from the freedom that floods my heart. My 'good girl,' with all her careful planning and craving for controlled perfection, discovers another way to move through the world.

I sit for hours in that square, watching pilgrims emerge from their journeys. Some wobble in on blistered feet, others dance their final steps. Many collapse in tears like me, while others throw their arms wide to the sky in jubilation. Bagpipes play their welcome song as stories of triumph and transformation float around me in a dozen languages. A German grandmother in her 70s has walked three times my distance. Nearby, a young American woman with a strapped ankle rests, having fallen on day one but taken the bus ahead to wait for her friends. "There's always next year," she tells me with a grin. "The Camino teaches you to let go of the journey you planned and trust the one you're given."

Now when that familiar urge rises at home—that need to know exactly how something will end before I begin—I remember those yellow arrows along the Camino. They never pointed toward a perfect path. They simply suggested the next step. Sometimes, that's all we need to know: we're not there yet, but each step proves we were made for this journey of learning and growth.

TAP IT OUT

Showing Self-Compassion: Evolve It

You can turn the messiness of learning into the magic of growing. By tapping key meridian points (the same used in acupressure) on your body as you help your brain process what's unfolding, you can turn challenges into opportunities.

1. **Rate your feelings:** On a scale of 0 (not distressed) – 10 (extremely distressed), how are you feeling about the learning that's unfolding? What's your greatest fear about how you've navigating this learning?

2. **Start tapping:** As you lightly tap five to seven times on each of the meridian points shown below with your fingertips, say: "Even though I'm feeling scared [insert your fear], I'm moving through the messiness of learning just like everybody else." Complete three rounds of this tapping.

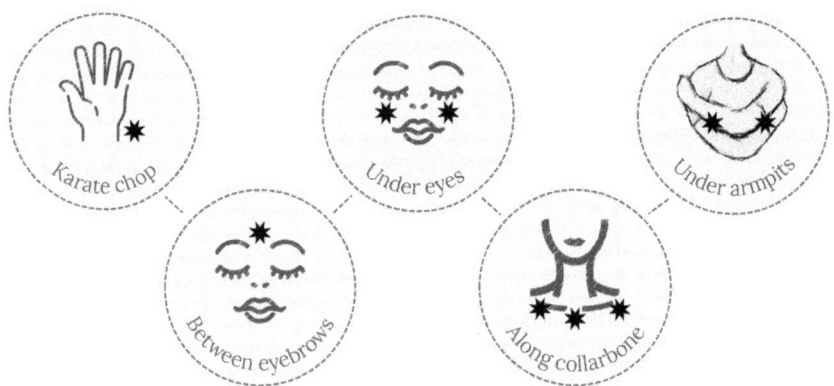

3. **Review your feelings:** How are you feeling now about the learning that's unfolding? Use the scale of 0 (not distressed) – 10 (extremely distressed) to observe any change. What are you learning about the process of growing?

Inspired by: Nick Ortner

RUN A LEARNING LOOP

Showing Self-Compassion: Evolve It

Accept that you're learning, just like everybody else. Make the time to unpack your strengths and your struggles. While most successes and failures fade, the lessons you learn will prepare you for future opportunities and hurdles. Use these prompts to help you self-compassionately journal or self-reflect on how you're doing:

1 What's working well?

Start with this question to identify your strengths and build your confidence. Even if it feels like nothing is working well, asking this question and being open to learning is a step in the right direction.

2 Where are you struggling?

There is no shame in struggling; it's your body's way of letting you know that important things are still being figured out. Even if everything seems fine, there is always room for continued growth.

3 What are you learning?

This is the key question. Imagine your wisest and kindest friend is reflecting on what you've shared about your strengths and struggles. What a-ha moments and actionable insights might they offer to support your growth?

4 What will you try next?

Tiny actions can have a mighty impact. Based on what you've learned what's the next tiny action you most want to take to continue growing?

Inspired by: Michelle McQuaid

TAKE A VICTORY LAP

Showing Self-Compassion: Evolve It

Researchers have found that celebrating your success is a powerful catalyst for change. It turns out that it's not repetition but emotions—particularly the feeling of intensely and authentically celebrating your progress—that build your confidence. Try these simple ways to savor your successes:

 Choose your celebration style: Pick what feels most natural and fun:

 Run a 'victory lap' on the spot

 Give yourself a pat on the back

 Do a little happy dance

 Smile as you declare Huzzah!

 Tick it off a list

 Share your good news

Amplify the good feelings: Once you've chosen your celebration, really let yourself enjoy it. Notice the feeling of joy and humble pride in your body. Savor this moment.

Make it a habit: Build a little celebration into your daily routine by celebrating your small wins, not just big achievements. Remember, taking time to celebrate isn't self-indulgent—it's how your brain learns to choose self-compassion over self-criticism more easily next time. The more you celebrate, the more natural it becomes.

Inspired by: BJ Fogg

Section 4 **Securely Attaching**

Chapter 10 **Securely Attaching Snapshot**

Our research revealed a deep conditioning that begins in childhood—the belief that a woman's primary role is to care for others. "As the older sister, you have to take care of your little brother; you have to be responsible," shared one participant, reflecting a common experience. More than 78% of respondents admitted they prioritized pleasing others to avoid rejection, often sacrificing their own needs. The message was consistent across experiences: to be loved and accepted, women must put others first, and prioritize everyone else's happiness above their own.

The toll of this conditioning is severe and multifaceted. Among those who reported prioritizing others over themselves, 67% expressed resentment about their sacrifices, and nearly 60% struggled to trust others. Women described feeling "exhausted," "spread too thinly," and "taken advantage of." "When I do something for myself, I feel guilty," one participant shared, while another noted, "I get resentful of others who don't seem quite so burdened by the responsibilities." As one woman summed it up, "I'm expected to put others first, conform, do the work at the expense of myself." These findings reveal a painful truth: women's attempts to secure love through self-abandonment not only exhaust them but create barriers to genuine connection, foster resentment, and erode emotional security in their relationships.

But our bodies know better. They've been whispering to us all along through symptoms we've been taught to ignore: the tension headaches, the stomach knots, the clenched jaws, the chronic fatigue. Each one a quiet rebellion against a world that demands our silence and sacrifice.

What if we stopped pathologizing these signals and started honoring them as sacred data? What if we met them not with frustration but with curiosity, reverence even? What if we recognized them for what they are—an ancient, evolutionary wisdom designed to protect us, connect us, perfect us?

This is the revolutionary invitation of secure attachment—not just in our external relationships, but in our internal ones too. It's the radical proposition that our relationship with ourselves forms the foundation for every other relationship in our lives. When we learn to tune into our bodies, honor our needs, and set kind and clear boundaries, not despite our yearning for belonging but because of it, everything changes.

These discoveries stem from our growing knowledge of the nervous system's primary operating modes. Every second of every day, our body performs an intricate dance between two essential circuits: one that pulls us toward connection and another that defends us from threat. This isn't just in our minds—it's in our biology. The vagus nerve, our body's longest cranial nerve, acts like a 24/7 surveillance system, constantly gathering data about safety and danger from our heart, lungs, gut, and facial muscles.

When this system detects safety signals—like warm eye contact, soothing voices, relaxed expressions—it switches on our connection circuit. This triggers a cascade of neurochemicals, including oxytocin (the bonding hormone that fosters trust and connection), serotonin (regulating emotions and wellbeing), and dopamine (rewarding positive interactions). This chemical flow allows us to stay present and engaged, forming the biological basis for genuine connection.

On the flip side, when this system senses threat, whether real or perceived, it shifts into protection mode. Our pulse quickens, breath shallows, and muscles tighten as we prepare to fight, flee, or freeze. Complex thinking and emotional nuance shut down as survival instincts take over. We become hyper-alert to potential danger, primed to react, and less able to access our innate capacity for connection and care—both for ourselves and others.

Grasping this biology illuminates why "just setting boundaries" often feels impossible when we're caught in our protection circuit's autopilot. As neuroscientist Stephen Porges found, when we're vigilant for social threats, our prefrontal cortex—the part of the brain that handles nuanced decisions—goes offline. We revert to primal survival patterns: people-pleasing, peacemaking, perfecting.

The good news? Therapists Dr. Ann Kelley and Sue Marriott show us how we can learn to notice and work with these nervous system cues rather than being ruled by them. They map our system states on a color spectrum:

- The *Green Zone* is our "just right" place, where we feel safe enough to stay rooted in our true self while meaningfully connecting with others. We experience relaxed alertness—an open, engaged curiosity paired with a settled nervous system. Our heart rate is steady, our breath is easy, our voice tone is warm, and our facial muscles are soft. We can access clear thinking, emotional balance, and attuned communication. The Green Zone isn't about being perfectly peaceful—it's about feeling secure enough to ride life's waves without losing our sense of self.

- The *Red Zone* is where we go when our system gets overheated by perceived social danger. Flooded by stress hormones, we frantically attune to others' needs while abandoning our own. Our heart races, our breath gets fast and shallow, our voice goes tight or shrill, and we feel restless, irritable, or anxious. Every mini disappointment feels disastrous; every boundary feels perilous. Caught in the Red Zone, we'll do almost anything to keep others happy and avoid rejection.

- The *Blue Zone* is where we go when our system tries to cool the overwhelming stimuli by shutting down and numbing out. In the Blue Zone, everything feels like too much effort. Our body gets heavy, our emotions flatten, our thinking fogs, and our voice goes monotone or robotic. We might take pride in "not being needy," but this icy self-containment comes at the cost of real connection—with others and ourselves. Camped out in Blue, we lose touch with our needs, wants, and feelings.

This leads to a crucial realization: Genuine safety in our outer relationships relies on cultivating secure attachment in our inner relationships first. When we can maintain the connection with our authentic needs and feelings even under pressure, we establish an unshakable foundation from which to engage others.

This is where skillful boundary-setting becomes vital—not to control others, but to practice trusting ourselves. As researcher Juliane Taylor Shore reveals, effective boundaries start inside, with micro-moments of honoring our felt experience. When we consistently validate our inner signals rather than overriding them, we build the base for clear, kind limits in our external relationships. This internal boundary work enables our nervous system to stay regulated, empowering us to remain present and real even in the face of others' disappointment or resistance.

Jane Fonda's path exemplifies this journey to secure self-attachment. "I was conditioned to please. I strived to become what my father wanted so he would love me," she explains. Throughout decades in the public eye, she openly discusses subordinating her true self to meet others' expectations—as a daughter, actress, wife, and activist.

"When you're severed from your body, you're severed from your emotions, severed from your authentic self," she notes. Studying trauma and attachment neuroscience, this insight crystallized—her chameleon-like adaptation wasn't a character defect but her nervous system's response to early unpredictability.

Her shift began as she started honoring her body's messages instead of hushing them. "At 60, I grasped that saying 'no' isn't selfish—it's how we preserve the energy for what truly matters," she reflects. She met her people-pleasing habits with new compassion, tuning in to what helped her physiology feel safe rather than forcing boundaries before she was ready.

Now, at 85, Jane models secure self-attachment in action. "The goal isn't perfection—it's wholeness. I wasted years conforming to others' wishes instead of discovering my own," she recently shared. Whether upholding boundaries around energy and time, voicing hard truths about climate, or standing firmly in her beliefs, she demonstrates what's possible when we learn to trust ourselves even if it disappoints others.

In this journal section, we'll explore science-backed practices to fortify our secure connection within. Using the F.R.E.E framework from Chapter 3, these tools will help you:

- **Feel It:** Learn to interpret your nervous system's cues and discern between actual danger and outdated protective patterns. Techniques like 'Check Your Safety Dial' will help you chart your unique nervous system terrain.
- **Release It:** Find practices to help your physiology feel safe enough to try new ways of being. Methods like 'Find the Floor' and 'Chop Through Grief' will help you metabolize the inherent losses in changing old patterns.
- **Experiment with It:** Test novel ways of staying true to yourself while crafting clear, caring boundaries. Tools like 'Set Healthy Boundaries' will help you practice respecting both your needs and your relationships.
- **Evolve It:** Expand your capacity for secure self-attachment through steady practice and self-reflection. Approaches like 'Build Boundary Muscles' will help you grow enduring faith in your ability to handle life's complexity while honoring your truth.

Remember, secure attachment isn't about attaining an ever-constant state of safety or sureness. It's about developing the inner resources to stay curious and connected to yourself even when you feel endangered or unsure. Some days, you'll uphold solid boundaries; other days, you'll slip into people-pleasing. What matters most isn't perfection but nurturing a relationship with yourself resilient enough to weather life's ups and downs while feeling empowered to learn and evolve.

FEEL IT

Check Your Safety Dial
Imagine a safety dial at the base of your head, that changes how your brain and body function. Is it telling you that you feel safe or unsafe?

Spot The ANTS
Are you being attacked by ANTS (automatic negative thoughts)? Can you spot these old stories and challenge them?

Show Up For Yourself
When you're feeling out of sorts, take the time you need to feel safe, seen, soothed, and secure.

RELEASE IT

Use Boundary PPE
Strengthen your sense of physical safety by creating boundaries that align with the space, touch, connection, time, and sound needs.

Find The Floor
Find a safe and quiet space to lie down on the floor. Take a deep breath in, then blow out any tension and let your body surrender fully.

Chop Through Grief
Release the grief that comes with setting boundaries, by using your body and breath to chop the grief and loss into manageable moments.

EXPERIMENT WITH IT

Set Healthy Boundaries
Clarify what is okay, isn't okay, and what you will do to keep yourself protected and connected with others if the not okay thing happens.

Build Psychological Safety
Create an image that safely catches people's judgments before they reach you. Ask yourself: True or not true? About me or not about me?

Act With Integrity
Surface your personal integrity word (who you want to be) and your relational integrity word (how you want to connect).

EVOLVE IT

Build Boundary Muscles
Help your brain build the muscles it needs to confidently stick with your boundaries using six evidence-based steps.

Rewire Attachment Patterns
Learn how to recognize, reflect, and rewire old attachment patterns, so you can learn how to trust yourself and others.

Repair Your Relationships
If you've messed up, remind yourself that you're still learning. Then apologize by taking responsibility and sharing what you'll change.

Chapter 11 **Securely Attaching – Feel It**

> we are **BRAVER** than we *Believe* OURSELVES TO BE

Fitting In
Evie's Story

The bleach burns my scalp like liquid fire. I am fourteen, gripping the salon chair, watching my mousy blonde hair disappear into a shade of acceptable. Four hours. Two hundred dollars. Every six weeks. This is the math of belonging.

My mother thinks this is teenage rebellion. It's not. Rebellion would be keeping my natural hair. Rebellion would be saying "no" to the weekly parties and staying in. Rebellion would be being myself.

But I am very busy becoming what everyone else needs me to be.

I learn there are rules to fitting in.

Your hair must be the right color (even if it's slowly snapping your hair off).

Your clothes must be new and exciting (even if they cost your savings).

Your weekends must be spent at the right parties (even if you don't want to go).

Your drink must be mixed with vodka (even if it makes you sick).

You must get a photo with the right group of girls (even if you don't even like them).

I get very good at this game. A master of the carefully curated performance. The popular girl. Watch me dissolve myself into acceptable pieces.

The problem with trying to fit in is that it works. For a while. People call you "pretty". They tell you you're "so cool." They invite you to places. And you begin to believe that this version of you—this bleached, dressed-up, watered-down mirage of yourself—is the only version worthy of love.

I spend three years of weekends in that salon chair. By the time my grade 12 formal rolls around, my hair can hardly stay in a bun it's so damaged. And my liver has seen more vodka shots than some people would see by 30. And I have no clue who the hell I am, but I know this isn't it.

Now, a decade later, I run my fingers through my natural hair and think about that girl in the salon chair. I want to tell her that belonging cannot be bought with a burned scalp and borrowed personality. I want to tell her that fitting in is not the same as being loved. I want to tell her that the very parts of herself she's trying to drink and party away are exactly what makes her worthy of loving.

But maybe she needed to learn it the slow way. Maybe we all do. Maybe there's no shortcut through the painful alchemy of transforming other people's expectations into your own truth. Maybe we all have to burn a little before we learn to trust our own light.

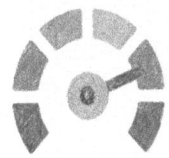

CHECK YOUR SAFETY DIAL
Securely Attaching: Feel It

By discovering how to support your nervous system as it fluctuates between your connection circuit (when you feel secure and want to bond with others) and your protection circuit (when you feel insecure and threatened by others), you can build the self-awareness and skills you need to stay grounded and connected. Imagine you're holding a dial and turning it to spot if you are in the:

Green Zone (just right): Your attachment system feels safe, enabling your connection circuit to draw you towards exploration, bonding, and belonging. This makes it easier to embody trust and love, even when relationships become challenging. Notice what makes it possible for you to hang out in this Zone and spend as much time here as you can.

Red Zone (too hot): Your attachment system feels threatened, causing your protection circuit to up-regulate and intensifying your attention, emotions, and actions. This makes everything feel urgent, causing you to abandon yourself in favor of pleasing or pleading with others. Notice what's triggered your fears in this Zone and try to take a cool pause to slow down your responses.

Blue Zone (too cool): Your attachment system feels vulnerable, causing your protection circuit to down-regulate and avoid emotional connections. This makes you scared that your relationships are demanding too much, so you protect yourself from honest conversations. Notice what's triggered your desire for separation in this Zone and ask for help.

Inspired by: Ann Kelly & Sue Marriott

SPOT THE ANTS
Securely Attaching: Feel it

Automatic Negative Thoughts (ANTS) start marching through your mind, they can leave quite a trail. But just like real ants, we can learn to spot these thought patterns and redirect them with self-compassion. This isn't about squashing every negative thought—it's about noticing when these little troublemakers are taking over and finding healthier paths for them to follow. For example:

Marching ANT	ANT-idote
I *never* get any help	I'm still learning to ask
Everyone else does it better	We're all works in progress
Everything is falling apart	Life has ups and downs
It's *all* my fault	I don't control everything
I'm *always* going to be alone	I can connect in little ways

Time to be an ANT-thropologist! Track your own automatic negative thoughts and create some ANT-idotes to help them march in a healthier direction:

Marching ANT	ANT-idote

Inspired by: Dr. Ann Kelly & Sue Marriott

SHOW UP FOR YOURSELF

Securely Attaching: Feel it

It takes real courage to admit when you're struggling, but in that moment of honesty, you reclaim your power to choose the path forward. Before you rush into action, take the time to remind yourself that you are:

SAFE	Reassure yourself that feelings of struggle are a normal and healthy part of learning and growth. Reach for self-compassion and be the wise and kind friend you need in this moment.
SEEN	Acknowledge the discomfort, confusion, and fear you may be experiencing. Don't rush to fix these feelings. Just sit and observe what is happening within you and around you.
SOOTHED	Calm your body and brain. Find the floor or a safe space to place your hands on your heart or belly and breathe deeply and slowly as your body softens.
SECURE	When you're feeling more secure, ask, "What do I need now? How do I want to go forward?" Accept you may need to sit for a while, ask someone for help, or take action.

Inspired by: Dr. Daniel Siegel & Tina Payne Bryson

Chapter 12 **Securely Attaching – Release It**

The Yes Girl
Evie's Story

"No worries!" It's my automatic reply, spoken before I can think.

A coworker needs help, a friend asks for advice late at night, a neighbor needs a favor—I always agree. I don't consider how tired I am, how much I've already given. This is who I've trained myself to be: The reliable one. The good one. The girl whose boundaries dissolve at the first sign of someone else's need.

Then, one Sunday evening, my closest friend texts asking to catch up. It's been a full-on week, and all I want is to soak in the tub until my fingers prune. I feel the familiar "yes, of course," rising in my throat—automatic, like breathing.

But this time, I pause. Maybe it's exhaustion, maybe it's something wiser, but I let myself sit with the hesitation.

In that pause, I notice things in my body: the weight in my chest, the tightness in my jaw, the way my shoulders have lived near my ears for weeks. For the first time, I let myself feel it all before I act.

"This week has been crazy, and I'm feeling a bit overwhelmed," I text back. "I need some time to recharge. Can we please take a rain check?"

I hit send and wait. The words glow on my screen. This is it. I've done it. I wait for the rejection, the disappointment, the subtle withdrawal of love I've spent my whole life trying to avoid.

But her response comes quickly, warm and gentle: "Of course. Take all the time you need. Love you ♥."

It's such a small moment, but it changes everything. A tiny crack in the facade of the always-available-girl I've built myself to be. Through that crack, something shifts, and I realize that maybe the greatest gift we can offer isn't our perpetual yes, but our honest truth.

I still catch myself slipping, offering yeses like apologies. The fear of disappointing others sits like a stubborn lump in my throat, making each "no" feel impossible to swallow. But on my braver days, I show up exactly as I am—in my truth.

Because I've learned that real connection doesn't grow from endless accommodation. It grows from the courage to be seen as we are—needs, limits, boundaries, and all.

FIND THE FLOOR
Securely Attaching: Release It

Lying on your back on the floor triggers your parasympathetic nervous system, which allows your body to rest, digest, and repair. From the moment your back finds the floor, you're letting your body know it is safe to surrender, which allows your muscles to relax and your breath to deepen. Even a few minutes on the floor is better than no minutes at all.

1. **Set a breath timer:** Use a free app like *iBreathe* to set a six-second chime. Studies suggest this is the most efficient rhythm for breathing.

2. **Choose a quiet, comfortable place to lie on the floor:** As soon as your back muscles touch the floor, notice how your body is feeling as you begin to breathe in and out in time with the six-second chime.

3. **Breathe into the floor:** As you continue breathing, observe the weight of your bones on the floor. Notice which of your rib bones connect to the floor. The next time you inhale, press your ribs gently into the floor. Then, as you exhale, let the ribs slowly release this pressure. Repeat this a few times, making it softer and softer. Then, rest for a few breaths.

4. **Breathe through your body:** When you're ready, repeat this same process through your shoulder blades, the back of your skull, your pelvis, calves, heels, and hands. Be sure to rest for a few breaths before moving to the next body part.

Inspired by: Nahid de Belgeonne

USE BOUNDARY PPE
Securely Attaching: Release It

Strengthen your sense of safety by creating physical boundaries that align with what your body needs. Use these PPE (Pause, Protect, Express) prompts to help you decide how close or far you want to be from others and what kind of touch you want or don't want.

1. **Pause:** When it's safe to do so take a moment to close your eyes, take several slow, deep breaths, and reassure your body that you are listening to what it needs and are here to support it.

2. **Protect:** Ask your body what kind of physical boundary it needs you to put in place. For example, it may be a boundary around:

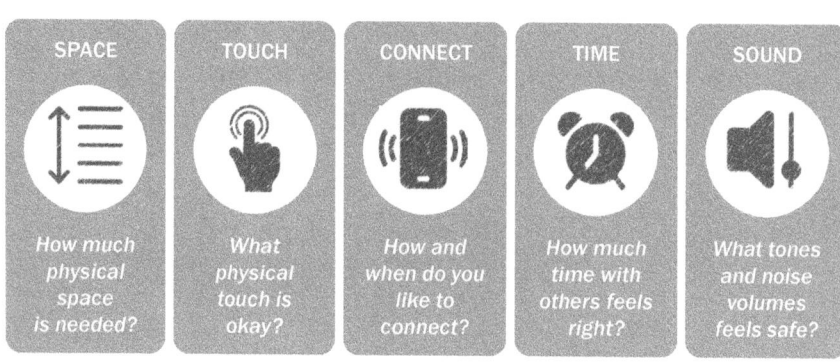

SPACE	TOUCH	CONNECT	TIME	SOUND
How much physical space is needed?	What physical touch is okay?	How and when do you like to connect?	How much time with others feels right?	What tones and noise volumes feels safe?

3. **Express:** Express your physical boundary in a way that is healthy for you and others. This prompt may assist: My brain is happiest when [insert your physical boundary]. I know everyone's a little different. Thanks for understanding.

Inspired by: Juliane Taylor Shore

CHOP THROUGH GRIEF
Securely Attaching: Release It

Setting boundaries is often accompanied by grief. We grieve that the boundary needs to be set, and we may grieve other people's responses. Trying to ignore, suppress, or numb grief can be problematic and damaging to our wellbeing. Instead, try this simple somatic practice of the wood chopper's breath:

Visualize the wood: Imagine a pile of wood in front of you, each piece representing a piece of your grief (i.e., anger for not being respected, fear at having to ask for what you need, sadness that your relationship will be different). Begin by taking a deep inhale through your nose and a long exhale out your mouth.

Chop the wood: Stand with your legs shoulder width apart and feet planted firmly on the ground. Clasp your hands together, making an axe with your thumb and index finger pointing upwards. Inhale, raising your arms above your head. As you exhale, swing your arms down as if you're chopping the wood, making a "HAA" sound as you exhale through your mouth. Repeat this step as much as you feel is needed.

Burn the wood: When you've released the grief you're holding, sit and breathe normally. Imagine lighting a soothing fire with the wood as a sense of acceptance, lightness, and peace settles within your body.

Inspired by: Tina Bruce

Chapter 13 **Securely Attaching – Experiment With It**

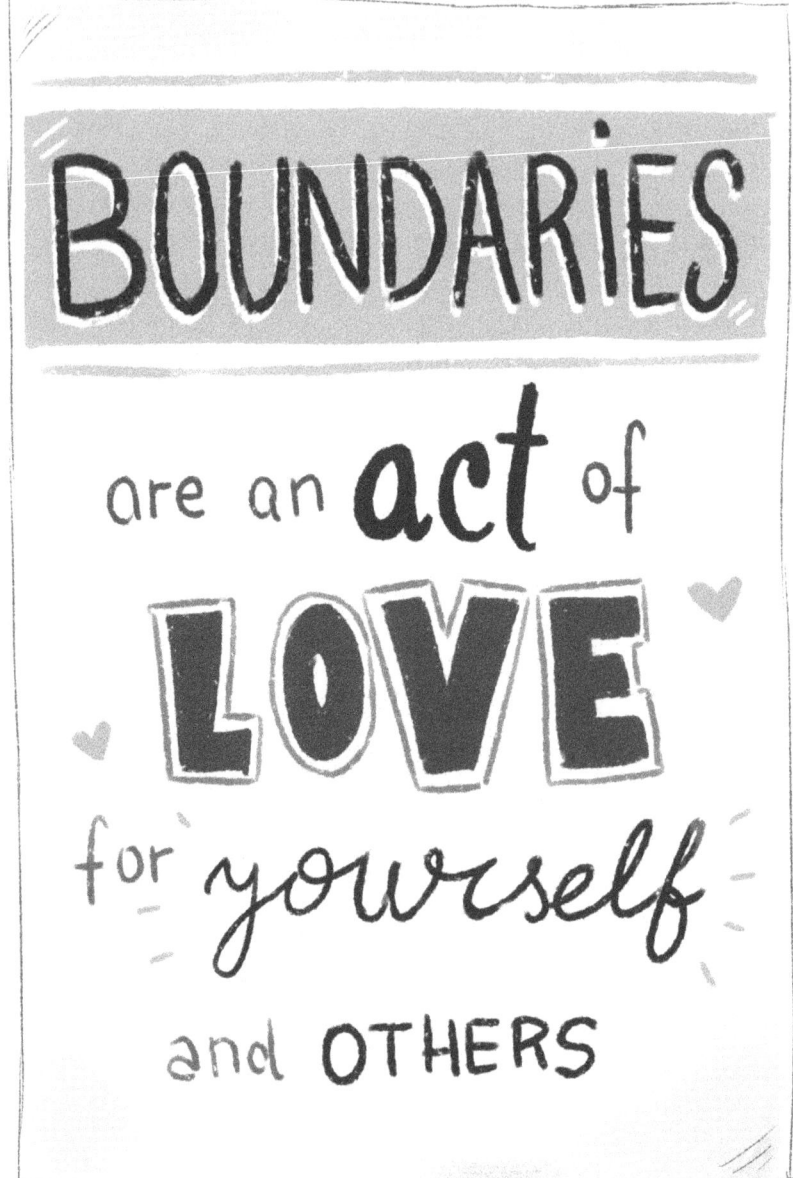

Running
Chelle's Story

The lighthouse beam sweeps across my windshield, matching the rhythm of waves crashing below. I've chosen this spot carefully—ninety minutes from home, location services disabled on my phone, cash withdrawn so my credit cards won't give me away. My husband thinks I'm at a conference in another city. After twenty years of marriage, I've become the kind of woman who leaves her own life.

"Nobody likes a difficult woman," whispers that familiar voice in my head. "Good girls stay. Good girls fix things." But here I am, forty-eight years old, my knuckles white against the steering wheel, finally choosing disruption over disappearing.

My truth unspools slowly over hours of silence and solitude. As my shoulders finally drop from their perpetual guard position, as my breath finally moves past the permanent knot in my chest, I begin to see how completely I've abandoned myself in the name of trying to be a 'good' wife.

Every day with my husband has become an exercise in emotional acrobatics. Will this be a moment of tenderness or tension? Will my request for time alone be met with understanding or accusations about taking what I'm not 'owed'? Will I be appreciated or scolded for being a disappointing wife and mother? I've tried to make myself smaller, quieter, more agreeable. But my body keeps score of every compromise, every swallowed truth, every moment I choose someone else's comfort over my own integrity.

The realization sits heavy in my chest. After nearly two decades together —some of these years genuinely happy—surely I can turn around, drive home, and find a way to keep going. For our children. For our shared history. For the 'good girl' in me who still wants to believe she can love someone enough to fix them.

But my body rebels against this familiar pattern of self-abandonment. My stomach clenches, my chest tightens, my throat closes around the very thought of returning to that constant vigilance, never knowing if the next moment brings an embrace or an explosion. It will not keep searching for salvation in someone else's conditional acceptance.

As the sun sets on my second day of hiding, I finally come to understand: I'm not running away from my marriage—I'm finally running towards myself. Towards the growing knowledge that I've lost touch with my own truth, my own needs, my own wisdom. Towards the growing acceptance that while I've been looking for someone else's love to save me, what I really need is to learn to stand securely in my own.

The kindest thing—for everyone—is to stop hiding. To own my choices, even the messy ones. To trust that I can handle the fallout of honesty better than the slow erosion of living out of integrity. To believe that real love never requires us to abandon ourselves.

So I turn my car towards home and the difficult conversations ahead. There will be years of careful untangling, of rebuilding what it means to be family without being husband and wife, of finding our way from who we've been to who we're becoming. Of learning that true security comes not from clinging to others but from finally, fully coming home to ourselves.

SET HEALTHY BOUNDARIES
Securely Attaching: Experiment With It

A healthy boundary clarifies what *you will do* to keep yourself protected and connected with others. You don't have to rely on anyone else to act a certain way or respect your limits. It is something you and you alone are in charge of. When you need to set a healthy boundary (for yourself or to share with others), it helps to be clear about:

1. The hurt: Honor your brain's need to feel safer in your relationships. Ask:
- What's happening in this situation that's making me feel hurt?
- What's the behavior I want to set a boundary around?
- Why is this boundary important to me?

It's not okay for _____.

2. The hope: Prompt your brain to stay curious and connected. Ask:
- What's happening in this situation that gives me hope?
- What's the behavior I value and want to prioritize?
- Why is this important for our relationship?

It is okay for _____.

3. The help: Reassure your brain it can trust and rely on you. Ask:
- What action am I willing to take when the not okay behavior occurs?
- Why is this action the healthy choice for me and others?
- How will this action reassure my body and brain that I am safe?

To take care of myself, I will _____.

Inspired by: Juliane Taylor Shore

BUILD PSYCHOLOGICAL SAFETY

Securely Attaching: Experiment With It

A psychological boundary protects us in ways that make it easier to stay compassionately connected with others who may feel disappointed, frustrated, angry, or hurt by the external boundaries we put in place. Using your brain's mentalization neural network can be an easy and effective way to DARE to create a safe space for yourself from the thoughts and feelings of others:

Discernment: Is it possible that the way other people think and feel is not always true and not always about you? Can you agree there is no need to take in what is not true or yours?

Acceptance: Is it respectful and compassionate to bear witness to other people's thoughts and feelings without trying to change them, control them, or deny them? Can you agree that it is kind to listen with acceptance to others?

Realization: Close your eyes and ask your heart and belly to show you an image that knows these two truths: It is kind to bear witness (listen with acceptance), and there is no need to take in what is not true or yours (discernment, seeing clearly). Let an image arise in your mind. Give this as much time as you need. Can you sketch it or jot down words that describe it?

Experimentation: Bring your psychological boundary image to mind when you need to create some space between you and the thoughts and feelings of others. For example, if someone calls you selfish, imagine your image (i.e., a wall of jello, a butterfly net, etc.) safely catching this accusation as you consider: Is this accusation true or not true? Is the accusation really about me or not about me?

Inspired by: Juliane Taylor Shore

SET HEALTHY BOUNDARIES
Securely Attaching: Experiment With It

A healthy boundary clarifies what *you will do* to keep yourself protected and connected with others. You don't have to rely on anyone else to act a certain way or respect your limits. It is something you and you alone are in charge of. When you need to set a healthy boundary (for yourself or to share with others), it helps to be clear about:

① The hurt: Honor your brain's need to feel safer in your relationships. Ask:
- What's happening in this situation that's making me feel hurt?
- What's the behavior I want to set a boundary around?
- Why is this boundary important to me?

It's not okay for _____.

② The hope: Prompt your brain to stay curious and connected. Ask:
- What's happening in this situation that gives me hope?
- What's the behavior I value and want to prioritize?
- Why is this important for our relationship?

It is okay for _____.

③ The help: Reassure your brain it can trust and rely on you. Ask:
- What action am I willing to take when the not okay behavior occurs?
- Why is this action the healthy choice for me and others?
- How will this action reassure my body and brain that I am safe?

To take care of myself, I will _____.

Inspired by: Juliane Taylor Shore

BUILD PSYCHOLOGICAL SAFETY

Securely Attaching: Experiment With It

A psychological boundary protects us in ways that make it easier to stay compassionately connected with others who may feel disappointed, frustrated, angry, or hurt by the external boundaries we put in place. Using your brain's mentalization neural network can be an easy and effective way to DARE to create a safe space for yourself from the thoughts and feelings of others:

Discernment: Is it possible that the way other people think and feel is not always true and not always about you? Can you agree there is no need to take in what is not true or yours?

Acceptance: Is it respectful and compassionate to bear witness to other people's thoughts and feelings without trying to change them, control them, or deny them? Can you agree that it is kind to listen with acceptance to others?

Realization: Close your eyes and ask your heart and belly to show you an image that knows these two truths: It is kind to bear witness (listen with acceptance), and there is no need to take in what is not true or yours (discernment, seeing clearly). Let an image arise in your mind. Give this as much time as you need. Can you sketch it or jot down words that describe it?

Experimentation: Bring your psychological boundary image to mind when you need to create some space between you and the thoughts and feelings of others. For example, if someone calls you selfish, imagine your image (i.e., a wall of jello, a butterfly net, etc.) safely catching this accusation as you consider: Is this accusation true or not true? Is the accusation really about me or not about me?

Inspired by: Juliane Taylor Shore

ACT WITH INTEGRITY
Securely Attaching: Experiment With it

When strong emotions arise in relationships, containing boundaries help you pause, feel, and respond with intention rather than reaction. By choosing specific words and gestures to anchor you, you can stay true to yourself while maintaining meaningful connections with others:

1. **Find your personal integrity word:**
   Ask: "Who do I want to be in my relationships, even when things get hard?" Choose one word (e.g., authentic, brave, compassionate, dignified) that reminds you of your deepest truth.

   My personal integrity word

2. **Choose your relational integrity word:**
   Ask: "How do I want to connect with others, even during conflict?" Pick one word (e.g., kind, respectful, honest, clear) that guides how you'll engage with others.

   My relational integrity word

3. **Create your self-compassion gesture:**
   Choose a gentle anchor (hand on heart, self-hug, peace sign) to help you pause, breathe, and show yourself kindness.

   My self-compassion gesture

Inspired by: Juliane Taylor Shore

Chapter 14 **Securely Attaching – Evolve It**

Selfish
Chelle's Story

I'm standing in my kitchen, wooden spoon frozen mid-stir, when my mother's words slice through the phone: "How can you be so selfish?" Just like that, I'm four years old again, kneeling beside my bed for nightly prayers, begging God for forgiveness. Because in my family, "selfish" isn't just a character flaw-it's a spiritual death sentence. The path to eternal damnation begins with putting yourself first.

My mother isn't trying to be cruel-she's trying to keep me safe in the only way she knows how, protecting me with the same walls that once sheltered her. Good girls give themselves away piece by piece: at church, in the community, to anyone who asks.

But somehow, my "selfishness" keeps showing up like a stain I can't wash out:

At five, playing hide-and-seek while my mother is late for work: "Stop being so selfish!"

At eleven, wanting to see my estranged father: "Why are you being selfish?"

At sixteen, leaving home because I no longer trust my mother's choices: "This is the most selfish thing you've ever done!"

At thirty-two, moving my young family across the world for my dream job: "Only ever thinking about yourself."

At forty-two, spending time with my dying father: "How could you selfishly hurt me like this?"

At forty-five, trying to heal the final pieces of my childhood trauma: "Why do you selfishly insist on dragging up the past?"

Each time, her cry of "selfish" slices through my carefully constructed peace, and I scramble to stitch myself back together with good deeds.

More service. More sacrifice. More giving myself away until she deems me lovable again.

Then, at forty-six, I finally set a boundary of silence with my mother. In the two years of quiet that follow, I discover something revolutionary: What feels like sin from the outside is actually salvation from within. I'm not being selfish—I'm finally showing up for myself with the same fierce devotion I once reserved for everyone else.

So, here's what I've learned about setting healthy boundaries: When people call you selfish, they're often really saying, "How dare you choose yourself over my comfort." They're saying, "Hey, your growth threatens my safety." They're saying, "Damn you, your healing forces me to look at my own wounds."

Of course, the word "selfish" still gets thrown my way, usually by people who still think women should sacrifice themselves for others' comfort. But now I hear it differently: not as a verdict, but as verification that I'm honoring my own needs. Because sometimes being "selfish" is actually being sacred—it's drawing a circle of light around your own heart and saying, "This too is holy ground."

BUILD BOUNDARY MUSCLES
Securely Attaching: Evolve It

Setting boundaries can be hard because our brains are designed to avoid discomfort. We often struggle to see how short-term choices not to upset people can come with long-term costs for our wellbeing. To help your brain build the muscles it needs to confidently set boundaries, try these six steps:

1. **Find Your Big Why:** What benefits might be gained by setting your boundary? What are the costs of not asking for what you need?

2. **Define Your Boundary:** What is okay for you in this situation? What is not okay? How will you respond if the not-okay things happen?

3. **Anticipate Other's Responses:** What visual mental can help you create a safe space image (i.e., a jello wall or butterfly net) to listen with acceptance and discern what is true or not true, about you or not about you, when it comes to people's responses to your boundary?

4. **Anticipate Your Reactions:** What personal integrity word can remind you of who you want to be (i.e., courage)? What relational integrity word can remind you of how you want to connect with others (i.e., kindness)?

5. **Create A Self-Soothing Plan:** Is there a soothing movement you can do (i.e., hand on heart) to help you remember that you're a good person facing a hard situation like all people have to?

6. **Say It and Follow Through:** What's a short, kind, and clear way to share with others what is okay, what isn't okay, and what you will do if the not-okay thing happens in the future?

Inspired by: Juliane Taylor Shore

REWIRE ATTACHMENT PATTERNS

Securely Attaching: Evolve It

When past experiences of emotional or physical neglect, danger, or loss have left your nervous system's protection circuits on high alert, you can learn to rewire these patterns. Use these three steps to help your brain encode new, safer experiences of trust and love:

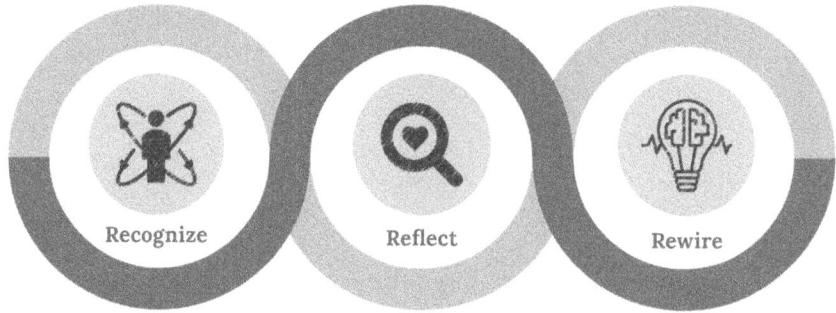

1. **Recognize:** Notice when your protection circuits are triggered, and you're feeling scrambled or frozen. What triggered my feelings? What sensations am I noticing in my body right now? What thoughts or fears are coming up for me?

2. **Reflect:** Pause to reflect with curiosity and compassion. Imagine your wisest and kindest friend helping you unpack the experience. How has my past shaped this response? What story am I telling myself right now? What would my wisest friend advise me to do?

3. **Rewire:** Take small steps to embody trust and love, starting with yourself. What small action can I take to support myself right now? How can I embody feelings of trust and love in this moment? Where in my life do I feel safest to practice connecting (i.e., your pets, your garden, your family, your friends, your community)?

Inspired by: Ann Kelly & Sue Marriott

REPAIR YOUR RELATIONSHIPS

Securely Attaching: Evolve It

If you've messed up, remind yourself that you're still learning—we all are. True repair with others happens when we take responsibility, authentically apologize, share what we'll change, and commit to growing together. The below journal prompts might help you M.E.N.D your relationships:

1. **Mindfully reflect:** What happened that you wish you'd handled differently? How have your actions affected the other person? What unmet needs or fears might have driven this behavior?

2. **Express responsibility:** Own your part in what happened and apologize. Name your impact clearly without defending or excusing. Show that you understand their feelings.

3. **Name your commitment:** Share specifically what you'll do differently. Make promises you can keep.

4. **Do the work:** Follow through with your commitments. Notice and celebrate the moments of connection.

In this situation, I recognize that I _____,
and this impacted you by _____.
I felt _____,
I'm sorry for _____.
I understand this hurt you because _____.
Moving forward I commit to _____,
and my first step will be _____.

Inspired by: Becky Kennedy

Section 5 **Strengthening Self-Leadership**

Chapter 15 **Self-Leadership Snapshot**

Our research revealed how the pressure to protect others through silence becomes ingrained early in life. Women described being conditioned to "be the peacemaker," "be accommodating," "never upset people," "don't cause conflict," "stay quiet," and "don't show emotions, especially anger." Over 67% of respondents admitted they often silenced their true feelings to avoid being abandoned, caught between their deep longing to speak their truth and their fear of the consequences.

The impact of this silencing is profound and far-reaching. Women reported feeling "invisible," experiencing "internal conflict," and living with a persistent "sense of emptiness," with 53.6% feeling they were not the person they wanted to be. Some turned to alcohol to numb their pain, while others remained in diminishing jobs or relationships, unable to voice their needs. Yet there are signs of resilience and hope—51.9% reported courageously speaking up when they needed to be true to themselves, 56% found some sense of real purpose in their lives, and 69.2% felt loved by important people for who they really are, suggesting that breaking free from silence, while challenging, opens the path to greater authenticity and fulfillment.

Internal Family Systems (IFS) research helps us understand the neurobiology underlying these patterns. IFS, developed by Dr. Richard Schwartz, proposes that our minds are composed of various "parts" or sub-personalities. When we experience chronic stress or trauma at a young age, parts of us step forward to shield our most vulnerable feelings, called our "exiles."

Some parts become "managers," who are proactive protectors that work to control situations and prevent painful feelings from being triggered. They are often perfectionistic, controlling, critical, and incessant in their attempts to keep us functioning through constant "shoulding," which can leave us feeling exhausted.

Other parts become "firefighters," who are reactive protectors that rush in when managers fail to keep painful feelings at bay. They are often impulsive and use extreme coping mechanisms like food, alcohol, drugs, sex, media, or work to numb the pain, which can have harmful consequences and often clash with the controlling efforts of managers.

While the intentions of managers and firefighters are positive, their protective strategies can leave us feeling fragmented, exhausted, and voiceless. These feelings can lead us to believe that these parts are "bad." However, rather than being inherently destructive, these parts take on extreme roles as a way to cope with and protect us from overwhelming experiences.

Yet beneath these protective patterns lies what Richard discovered through decades of clinical work: each person has a natural capacity for clear, compassionate leadership, which he termed "Self-energy." This Self cannot be damaged or destroyed—it simply gets obscured by our protective parts, like clouds covering the sun.

When we strengthen our Self-energy, we gain more access to eight important capabilities:

- **Calm:** Being centered and grounded, even during stressful circumstances.
- **Curiosity:** Being genuinely open to learning why you and others react the way they do.
- **Clarity:** Maintaining a clear and undistorted view of situations and yourself without projections and agendas.
- **Compassion:** Seeing through challenging behavior to the pain that is driving it.
- **Creativity:** Being free to realize creative potential, enjoyment, and exploration.
- **Confidence:** Trusting that even if you have made mistakes, you are still good and worthy.
- **Courage:** Facing fearful situations, standing up to things that are not right, speaking for yourself, and apologizing for any negative impact on other people.

- **Connectedness:** Feeling a sense of interdependence with all the different parts of yourself, as well as external people and systems.

Neurologically, when we slow down to listen to our body's signals, explore movement with curiosity rather than judgment, and honor our nervous system's needs, we create space for our natural Self-energy to emerge. Our breath deepens, our muscles relax, and our thinking becomes clearer. Rather than being hijacked by protective patterns, we can integrate our full range of resources. This integration enables us to respond thoughtfully rather than react reflexively, to hear our own truth while remaining connected to others, to lead from wisdom rather than wound.

"Once you can reduce your emotions to biological processes, it's so liberating because then it means that you're not broken, you're not defective, you don't need to be fixed, you just need to tend to yourself," explained somatic movement educator Nahid de Belgeonne.

Singer-songwriter Alanis Morissette's journey with IFS illustrates this path. Despite her professional success, she struggled for years with anxiety, eating disorders, and a deep disconnection from herself.
"I was the classic 'good girl' overachiever," she explained. "I'd show up perfectly, perform perfectly, and make sure everyone else was perfectly comfortable—while inside, I was falling apart."

Through IFS work, she began recognizing how different parts of herself had developed to cope with early expectations and trauma. Her perfectionist manager part tirelessly drove her toward achievement. Her people-pleasing part worked overtime to keep everyone happy. Her firefighter parts sought relief through work addiction and disordered eating.

"What changed everything was learning that these weren't enemies to eliminate, but parts of me trying their best to help," Morissette shared. "When I could meet them with curiosity instead of judgment, something profound shifted. I could finally hear my own voice—not just the voices of what everyone else wanted me to be."

This integration of her parts allowed Morissette to create from a deeper place of authenticity. Her 2020 album "Such Pretty Forks in the Road" openly explores her journey of healing and self-discovery. "The songs came from my Self—that place of clarity and compassion that can hold all the parts of who we are," she noted. "It's not about being perfectly healed. It's about having the courage to show up exactly as you are."

The path forward isn't about eliminating our protectors but helping them trust that our Self can now show up with the wisdom and care they've tried so hard to provide. In this section, you'll find evidence-based practices designed to strengthen your Self-leadership capabilities using our F.R.E.E framework:

- **Feel It:** Learn to recognize when your protective parts are activated and reconnect with your Self-energy. Tools like "Find Your Self" and "Map Your Protectors" help you notice when parts are taking over so your Self-energy can help.

- **Release It:** Calm your nervous system when you're feeling overwhelmed so your Self-energy can emerge. Practices like "Take A You-Turn" and "Soothe Your Protectors" offer ways to settle your protectors.

- **Experiment with It:** Build trust with all aspects of yourself so you can lead from Self-energy more often. Tools like "Move Toward Your Parts" and "Meet Your Exiles" help you connect with protectors and heal exiles.

- **Evolve It:** Expand your capacity for self-leadership over time by strengthening your Self-energy. Practices like "Accessing Self" and "Unburdening Ceremony" help you embody your compassion, curiosity, clarity, courage, confidence, creativity, calm, and connectedness.

Choose the practices that resonate with your current needs. Some days, you'll find it easier to access Self-energy; other days, protective parts will step forward strongly. This rhythm of expansion and contraction is natural—what matters is maintaining gentle curiosity about what each aspect of you needs to feel safe enough to relax into your Self's leadership.

FEEL IT

Find Your Self
When have you shown up as your wisest and kindest Self? Find a visual image, phrase, or a gesture that can remind you this Self energy is within you.

Map Your Protectors
As you move through your day notice the strong emotions, thoughts, beliefs, urges, and sensations you experience with compassion and curiosity.

Meet Your Exiles
When you've built trust with your protectors gently ask: "Who are you protecting? Can I meet them please?" Respect your protector's choice.

RELEASE IT

Take A You-Turn
If you're feeling overwhelmed, pause and turn inward with curiosity and compassion. Ask your part/s to step back a little so your Self energy can help.

Soothe Your Protectors
Ask: Where does this emotion, thought, belief, urge or sensation feel in my body? Place your hands there and breathe in Self energy.

Offer A Butterfly Hug
Cross your wrists so palms face your chest and interlock your thumbs. Gently tap your open hands on your chest for 20 seconds. Repeat as needed.

EXPERIMENT WITH IT

Strengthening Your Self
Try to connect with your Self energy each day. Meditate, visualize, journal, walk, or sit in nature. How do you like to connect with Self?

Move Towards Your Parts
Notice your parts with compassion and curiosity. Take the time to get to Know them. Listen to what they Need to feel supported by you.

Re-Do The Past
Ask your exile parts to share what hurt them in the past and how they would like help re-doing what occurred. Imagine taking these steps together.

EVOLVE IT

Accessing Self
Wrap your arms gently around your body in a big warm hug. Thank your Self energy for its unconditional support.

Check In On Your Parts
Take your parts for a walk, meditate together, or journal regularly. Ask: Who needs to be heard? What do you need me to know? Then, listen.

Unburdening Ceremony
As your exile part unburdens from the pain of their past, co-create a meditative ceremony to release their old beliefs, emotions, and sensations.

Chapter 16 **Self-Leadership – Feel It**

within each of us BURNS the FLAME of KINDNESS

Silence
Chelle's Story

I am four years old, pressed close against my sister in the bottom of our wardrobe. We are becoming experts at this: the holding of breath, the counting of heartbeats, the art of becoming so small we might dissolve into the darkness. Outside, our father's drunken rage fills every corner of the house. Inside our hideaway, we learn the first lesson of being 'good girls': how to silence our truth.

No one talks about these nights. Not about the screaming that makes the walls shake. Not about the bruises on our mother's skin. Not about how children shouldn't know exactly how many breaths they can take before they start to make noise. We learn instead what good girls do: Keep secrets. Stay quiet. Protect others by silencing your own pain. Never, ever become a 'melodramatic drama queen.'

My mother teaches us this to protect us—terrified that if anyone knows what happens in our home, they'll take us away. Now, decades later, I understand how a mother's love can become a daughter's prison. How the fear of speaking up teaches us that survival means smoothing over the cracks of other people's bad behavior, no matter the cost.

These lessons of silence follow me for thirty years. When my high school teacher makes sexual advances, I say nothing. 'Good girls' don't make a scene. When my boss throws a stapler at my head for a typo, I pick it up and hand it back with an apology. 'Good girls' don't challenge authority. When my partner kicks me in the ribs, I cover my bruises and don't make a fuss. 'Good girls' protect the people they love.

I become so good at making ugly things look okay. So good at turning other people's pain into my own deepest shame. So good at keeping secrets in the desperate hope that my silence will finally earn me someone's love.

Then comes the moment that cracks everything open. My younger sister, trembling at thirty years old, stands before our dying father and tells her truth: he sexually abused her throughout childhood. He calls her a liar. Calls her crazy. Calls her a drug addict. And for the first time in my life, my silence feels like betrayal rather than love.

Because I know. I know the weight of the secret she carries. I know because I carry the same secret from my own childhood. I know what happens to a little girl's heart, mind, and body when our silence protects the wrong person.

So I open my mouth. Decades of carefully guarded secrets spill out. I choose to stop being good. Choose my sister's wellbeing over keeping quiet. Choose truth over protection. Choose to believe that real love never demands our silence.

This is what society's 'good girl' training costs us: the belief that protecting others means sacrificing ourselves. That staying quiet about abuse makes us good rather than complicit. That smoothing things over matters more than speaking up.

But our bodies hold a different knowing. When we dare to break our silence, we discover our voice—however shaky and afraid—becomes our most powerful tool for creating genuine safety, connection, and change.

Find Your Self

Strengthening Self-Leadership: Feel It

When have you shown up as your wisest and kindest Self? The good news is we all have moments when we're courageous, curious, compassionate, clear, calm, confident, creative, and connected (the Internal Family Systems 8C capabilities of Self). To strengthen your connection to your Self-energy, try our S.E.L.F reflection:

1. **Sit:** Place one hand on your heart and one hand on your belly. Take in a slow, easy breath to where you can feel your hands resting. Continue breathing gently here until you feel calm and grounded in your body.

2. **Explore:** When you're ready, think back to a time when you showed up as the wisest and kindest version of Self for others and/or yourself. A time when you had no agenda, just genuine care and love.

3. **Listen:** As you think about this moment and what unfolded, can you recall how you drew on your capacities for: Courage? Curiosity? Compassion? Creativity? Clarity? Calm? Confidence? Connectedness? Which of these Self capacities most resonate with you?

    My strengths are _____.

4. **Find:** As you sit with this wisest and kindest version of your Self and recognize these capabilities within you, is there a visual image, a word or phrase, a gesture, or a name that can remind you that this Self-energy is always there to be accessed?

    My Self is found by: _____.

Inspired by: Michelle McQuaid

Map Your Protectors
Self-Leadership: Feel It

Our protective parts develop to keep us safe, but their strategies can become rigid or overwhelming. Using M.A.P. (Meet, Acknowledge, Provide), you can better understand and support your parts with curiosity and compassion.

① Meet your parts: As you move through your day, notice which protective parts arise. Here are some common examples:

THE PLEASER
Seeks approval of others by putting their needs first.

THE ACHIEVER
Highly driven and focused on success.

THE AVOIDER
Procrastinates and delays challenging tasks to feel safe.

THE SOOTHER
Keeps the peace to avoid conflict in relationships.

THE CHARMER
Wins people over by making them laugh and feel good.

THE ESCAPIST
Numbs stress, pain, or boredom with addictions.

② Acknowledge their roles: For each of your parts, identify if it's a:

MANAGER
Tries to maintain control to prevent emotional pain.

FIREFIGHTER
Reacts to triggers by distracting from discomfort.

EXILE
Holds past wounds and vulnerable emotions.

③ Provide support: For each part you've identified:

THANK
Thank your parts - they're trying to protect you.

ASK
What are you afraid would happen if you didn't help?

LISTEN
What support does your part need to feel safe?

Inspired by: Richard Schwartz

Meet Your Exiles
Strengthening Self-Leadership: Feel It

When you've built trust with your protectors and they're willing to let you meet the parts they're protecting, use these gentle journal prompts to get to meet your exiles with curiosity and compassion. Move slowly, stay gentle, and respect if your exile needs space. Like building trust with a wounded child, this process requires patience, consistency, and deep compassion.

LISTEN IN
- What feelings or sensations arise in your body when you think about this exile?
- Can you get an image or sense of what this exile looks like?
- Where in your body does this exile seem to be located?

LEAN CLOSER
- What is this exile afraid might happen if it shares its story?
- What does this exile need from you to feel safe to open up?
- How can you show this exile you're here to listen without judgment?

LEARN MORE
- Can this exile share a memory or image of when it first felt this way?
- How did this experience make the exile feel at that time?
- What does this exile believe about itself because of this experience?
- If it could speak freely, what would it want to tell me now?

LOVE DEEPLY
- What did this exile need but never receive in the past?
- What positive qualities might emerge if it could release its burdens?
- How can you help this exile feel seen, heard, and valued?
- What support does this exile need from you going forward?

Inspired by: Richard Schwartz

Chapter 17 **Self-Leadership – Release It**

Shape Shifter
Evie's Story

I am eight years old, sitting cross-legged on the cold kitchen linoleum, my stomach twisted into knots as my parents' voices slice through the walls. I don't fully understand what they're fighting about, but I understand my role with crystal clarity: I need to fix this.

"Dad didn't mean it like that," I explain to my tearful mother.

"Mom's just tired," I tell my frustrated father.

"Everything will be okay if we just..." I promise them both.

Little me, desperately trying to smooth over every ripple of tension, every hint of discord. I learn fast that peace comes at a price, and I'm willing to pay it. Every time.

By twelve, I'm fluent in the language of other people's emotions. I can sense my mum's moods before she can. I know exactly which questions will make her soften, which words will pull her back when she's angry. I know when my dad is sad and what I need to say to cheer him up.

I am a shapeshifter, morphing into whatever they need: therapist, mediator, peace-keeper, good little girl.

No one taught me this directly. It came in the air I breathed, in every 'good girl' story I'd ever heard: girls fix things, girls make peace, girls sacrifice themselves to keep others comfortable.

Into my adult years, my nervous system becomes a finely tuned instrument, always scanning for the slightest shift in mood, the smallest sign of discord. I learn to read rooms before entering them, to anticipate needs before they're spoken, to jump in at the first hint of tension and fix, fix, fix.

What I don't see, in all my frantic fixing, is how this hypervigilance reshapes me.

Every time I cushion someone else's emotional landing, I'm not just protecting them—I'm teaching them they don't need to learn to stand on their own. While I'm busy protecting everyone else from life's necessary struggles, I'm the one hitting the ground. Over and over and over.

It takes me thirty years to understand that my family's emotions were never mine to control. That little girl on the kitchen floor wasn't failing when she couldn't manage everyone's feelings—she was just doing the only thing she knew to feel safe.

Sometimes, love means watching people you care about struggle without rushing in to save them. Sometimes, the kindest thing you can do is trust that they have their own path to walk, their own lessons to learn, their own strength to find. You can care without trying to save. You can love without carrying the pain.

The path to freedom isn't in perfecting our ability to save others—it's in finally, mercifully, putting down that impossible job and learning that we were never meant to be anyone's emotional shapeshifter.

Take A You-Turn
Strengthening Self-Leadership: Release It

If you're feeling overwhelmed by strong emotions, pause and make a You-turn inward with curiosity and compassion. This simple practice helps create space between your reactive parts and your Self-energy.

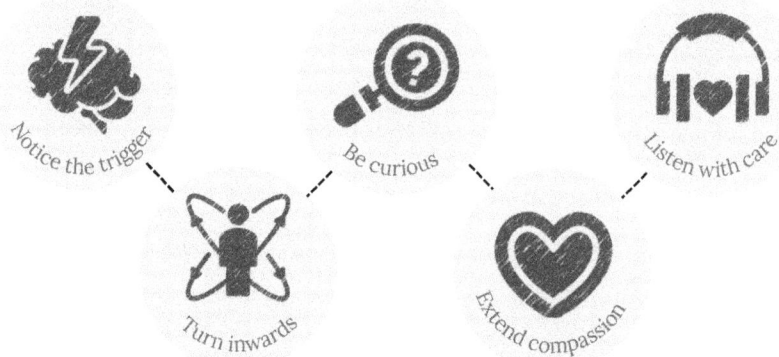

1. **Notice the trigger:** When you're overwhelmed or reacting strongly, pause and take a slow, deep breath. This is your signal that a part needs attention. When you feel triggered or overwhelmed, pause and take a slow breath. Some part of you needs attention.

2. **Turn inwards:** Place one hand on your heart, one on your belly. Let your shoulders drop and jaw soften.

3. **Be curious:** Ask gently, "What part of me is feeling triggered right now?" Notice where you feel this in your body.

4. **Extend compassion:** Say, "I see you're trying to help protect me. Would you be willing to step back just a little so our Self-energy can help?"

5. **Listen with care:** Take slow breaths as you wait for this part to respond. Notice if you can access your Self's curiosity or compassion.

Inspired by: Richard Schwartz

Soothe Your Protectors
Strengthening Self-Leadership: Release It

When we're struggling, parts of us often feel restless or upset within our bodies—maybe a tightness in our chest, a churning stomach, or tension in our shoulders. These are our protectors trying their best to keep us safe. This gentle conversation can help them trust that your Self-energy can now care for you in new ways.

1. **Connect to your Self:** Take several slow breaths and notice if you can feel any warmth, openness, or caring towards this protector. Place your hands where you feel this part in your body. Only proceed when you sense your calm, curious Self is present.

2. **Listen to your protector:** Invite your protector part to complete these statements in whatever way feels true for them:

    I'm showing up right now because _____.
    My job in your life has been to _____.
    I learned to protect you this way when _____.
    What scares me most is _____.
    What I really need from you is _____.
    I would feel safer if _____.
    Could you help me by _____.

3. **Build trust slowly:** Don't rush this conversation. Check that you maintain Self-energy throughout. If your protector isn't ready to share everything, thank it for what it could tell you and let it know you're here whenever it needs you.

Inspired by: Richard Schwartz

Offer A Butterfly Hug
Strengthening Self-Leadership: Release It

When you're feeling overwhelmed or distressed, this simple bilateral stimulation technique can help calm your nervous system and bring your Self-energy back online. Like giving yourself a gentle butterfly hug, this practice helps your protector and exile parts feel safer and more secure.

1. **Find your butterfly position:** Cross your arms over your chest, with your palms resting flat and your fingertips below your collarbones. Your thumbs can gently interlock, creating butterfly "antennae."

2. **Flutter your wings:** Begin alternately tapping your palms against your chest—left, right, left, right—as if your butterfly is gently fluttering its wings. Keep the pace slow and soothing.

3. **Take a few butterfly breaths:** As you continue tapping, imagine your butterfly wings moving in harmony with your breath. Let each exhale help your body soften and settle.

4. **Let your butterfly land:** After about 20 seconds of gentle tapping (or whenever it feels right), let your butterfly come to rest. Notice if your body feels calmer and more grounded.

Repeat these steps as often as needed, letting each butterfly hug remind your parts that they're safe and cared for.

Inspired by: Francine Shapiro

Chapter 18 **Self-Leadership – Experiment With It**

No Bad Parts
Chelle's Story

The night before my biggest presentation yet, I sit in my hotel room surrounded by note cards. Two thousand people will fill that auditorium tomorrow, and inside me, different parts of myself are spinning into their familiar protective patterns—each one trying to keep me safe in its own way.

My "teaching superstar" part has been running the show for weeks. She's a manager, one of those protective parts that tries to prevent any possible problem before it can occur. Right now, her presence feels like a tightly wound spring in my chest as she obsessively reviews my notes for the hundredth time. "One more rehearsal," she insists, though we've been at it for hours. "We can't risk anything going wrong tomorrow."

But her relentless drive for perfection has triggered another part of me—my "big spender," a firefighter part that rushes in whenever anxiety threatens to overwhelm. "Let's just check the Apple store," she suggests, already reaching for the laptop. "Maybe a new presentation clicker would help? Or we could still find a professional speech writer to rewrite everything overnight?" She's already nearly bankrupted my fledgling speaking business twice, desperately trying to spend away any trace of discomfort or doubt.

And somewhere deeper, curled into the pit of my stomach, my "little one" trembles. She's an exile, a young, vulnerable part of me that's been tucked away since childhood, carrying the weight of every time being seen felt dangerous, every moment vulnerability led to hurt. "Please," she begs, "can't we just call in sick and hide under the covers?"

Just months ago, I wouldn't have recognized these different aspects of myself—the manager frantically preparing, the firefighter ready to shop away our stress, the exile hiding from exposure. They emerged as chaos when I left my comfortable corporate career to share what I was learning about wellbeing science. I saw them as character flaws to eliminate: my teaching superstar "too controlling," my big spender "irresponsible," my little one "weak." I exhausted myself trying to silence them all, believing that destroying these broken pieces would finally make me whole.

Every presentation was a battlefield of competing needs: the call to make a difference wrestling with the terror of being seen, the drive for perfection clashing with the urge to run away. The more I fought against these parts of myself, the louder and more desperate they became.

But tonight feels different. As I sit cross-legged on the hotel bed, I consciously slow my breathing and feel my Self-energy emerge—that wise, grounded presence that comes online when my brain is integrated and free. "Hey everyone," I whisper to my parts, "I see how hard you're all working to keep us safe. Thank you."

The internal commotion stills, like children surprised by a kind teacher.

"Would you be willing to try something different tomorrow?" my Self continues. "You don't have to come out on stage if it feels too scary. You can wait in the wings where it's safe. I'll go out and guide us through this, then come right back for all your feedback. What do you think?"

My parts shift uncertainly. The teaching superstar shuffles her notes. The big spender's hand hovers over the laptop, ready to panic-purchase. The little one peeks out cautiously from her hiding place.

"I know you're not sure I can do this," my Self acknowledges. "But you're exhausted from trying to protect me in all your different ways. Just this once, let me show you what's possible when we trust ourselves."

Slowly, tentatively, they agree. My teaching superstar hands over her notes with a stern look that says, "Don't mess this up." My big spender reluctantly closes the laptop. My little one uncurls just enough to watch.

The next morning, I step onto the stage, not perfect but present. Not fearless but free. As I begin to speak, I feel my Self-energy flowing through me—curious about the audience, creative in responding to their energy, compassionate with any stumbles. The applause afterward is thunderous, but the real victory is in the wings where my parts wait with wide-eyed wonder.

"We did it," I tell them as we head back to the hotel. "All of us together."

Over time, my parts have learned to trust my Self-energy more and more. My teaching superstar still creates stellar presentations, but without the crushing pressure of perfection. My big spender has transformed her impulsive purchases into skilled financial management for our growing business. And my little one? She keeps me honest, grounded, and real—reminding me that our vulnerability is also our strength.

Instead of exhausting myself trying to silence them or fix them, I make space for their wisdom. Because each of these voices—even the ones that once terrified me—carries a truth about what it means to be human in front of two thousand watching eyes.

The real gift isn't in perfecting my performance or eliminating my fears. It's in discovering that I can show up fully, bringing all my parts with me—the worried ones, the wanting ones, the wounded ones. They're not distractions from my work; they are my work. Each time I step onto a stage now, I carry them with me like well-worn talismans, proof that our power lies not in being flawless, but in being whole.

They remain with me still, these parts of myself. Not bad or broken, just healing. Because true self-leadership isn't about silencing any of the voices within us—it's about learning to listen—really listen—to what each part is trying to tell me. Because our deepest wounds tend to point the way to our most important work.

Strengthening Your Self

*Strengthening Self-Leadership:
Experiment With It*

Your Self-energy—that wise, grounded presence within you—is like the sun: always there, even when hidden by clouds. This practice helps you discover your natural ways of parting those clouds to let your Self-energy shine through.

1 **Seek your path (5–10 minutes daily for a week):** Discover which practices most naturally clear the clouds for you. Try one approach each day:

SITTING	SEEING	SCRIBING	SENSING	STROLLING
Meditate to connect to your inner wisdom	Visualize light and warmth within you	Journal a conversation with Self	Breath gently as you scan your body	Walk mindfully in nature to connect

2 **Sense your Self-energy:** Which of these Self capabilities emerged?
- ☐ Curiosity: A genuine interest in discovering what unfolds
- ☐ Compassion: A warm, kind presence toward yourself
- ☐ Clarity: An undistorted view, free from judgment
- ☐ Calm: A centered, grounded, steadiness
- ☐ Courage: A readiness to face what arises
- ☐ Creativity: A natural flow of fresh possibilities
- ☐ Confidence: A trust in your inner wisdom
- ☐ Connectedness: A sense of being part of something larger

3 **Surface your insights:** At the end of the week, reflect: When did you feel most clear and grounded? How might you bring more of this light into your daily life?

Inspired by: Richard Schwartz

Move Towards Your Parts

*Strengthening Self-Leadership:
Experiment With It*

Rather than judging or fighting against your protective parts, try moving towards them with curiosity and compassion. Remember, your parts developed to protect you. They're not enemies to eliminate, but aspects of yourself waiting to be understood. Try this three-step process to help you connect with your parts from a place of Self-energy.

NOTICE

Be a gentle observer of your parts.
- Where in your body do you feel this part's presence?
- What thoughts, emotions, or sensations are arising?
- How are you feeling towards this part right now? (If you don't feel curious or compassionate, another protective part may need space.)

KNOW

Listen to your part's story with openness.
- What would you like me to know about why you're showing up now?
- When was the first time you felt you needed to protect me?
- What are you worried might happen if you didn't protect me in this way?

NEED

Offer your part genuine care and support.
- What do you need from me to feel less activated?
- How can my Self-energy help you feel safer?
- What would help you trust that I can handle things now?

Inspired by: Jenna Riemersma & Richard Schwartz

Re-Do The Past

*Strengthening Self-Leadership:
Experiment With It*

Although we can't change the past, we can help our wounded parts heal from it. Your exile parts tend to stay frozen in time, carrying the hurt and needs that went unmet into the future. By mindfully traveling back with your Self-energy, you can create a healing "do-over" that offers the protection, comfort, and support that was missing in those moments. At any point, if the journey feels too intense, pause and say, "Let's take a break in the present moment." Healing happens at your exile's pace.

1. **Prepare for the journey:** Place your hand on your heart and take three deep breaths to ground yourself. Then, ask your exile, "Would you like to show me when you got hurt?" Let your exile know you'll be a safe travel companion who can pause or return to the present anytime.

2. **Travel back together:** Let your exile guide you to its memory. Notice the sights, sounds, and feelings of that moment. What did this young part need help the most?

3. **Change the scene:** Ask your exile, "How can we make this moment different? What would help you feel safe and supported?" Let it direct the changes needed.

4. **Rewrite the story:** Like a protective guardian, step into that past moment. Offer what your exile needed—whether defending it from harm, speaking up, or wrapping it in comfort and understanding.

5. **Return home:** Invite your exile to travel forward with you to a safe place in the present—somewhere it can finally feel peaceful and protected.

Inspired by: Richard Schwartz

Chapter 19 **Self-Leadership – Evolve It**

Coming Home
Evie's Story

I'm twenty-nine, perched on a rattan yoga mat that's seen better days. My hands rest naturally where they always seem to find themselves lately—in a self-hug.

My yoga teacher's voice floats through the room: "Just notice what's here in this moment."

"You don't have to fix anything. You don't have to be or do anything," she adds.

I breathe slowly, feeling my hands rise and fall with each breath until the room steadies around me. Until I steady within myself. This is how I find my way back now—through the simple ritual of sitting with myself, exploring what's here, listening to what emerges.

Gosh, we've been through a bit, you and I, I think, and memory rises like a tide.

This body has weathered decades of striving and surviving. It's carried me through nights bent over deadlines, mornings dragging itself from bed before dawn, and countless moments of pretending everything was fine when it wasn't. It's held the weight of unspoken words, the ache of emotions swallowed whole, and the exhaustion of always trying to be enough.

But it's also carried me through moments of profound courage—when I shared my thoughts in an important meeting at work, my voice shaking but my heart steady and sure. Through moments of deep connection—when instead of running from hard conversations, I learned to stay present with myself and others, breathing through the discomfort. Through moments of surprising calm—finding stillness even in chaos, like holding space for my mother's grief without trying to fix anything, just being there, anchored in my own quiet strength.

When the world feels chaotic, when I need to remember who I really am, I return to those moments of courage, connection, and calm. They're not just memories—they're proof of my wisest, kindest Self. The Self that's always been here, waiting patiently beneath the noise of should-bes and not-enoughs.

I'm sorry, I think, not in the self-pitying way I once would have, but in the tender way you'd apologize to an old friend you've neglected. *I didn't know how to stay with you. But I'm here now.*

As class wraps up and people start rolling up their mats, I don't leave with a feeling of arrival—this journey of self-connection has no finish line, no final destination to reach.

Instead, I leave with a promise: to keep sitting with my Self in gentle attention, like you'd sit with someone you love. To keep exploring what arises with curiosity instead of judgment, like each feeling is a door waiting to be opened. To keep listening for the wisdom that's always been here, waiting to be heard beneath the static of everyday life.

Because being my authentic Self is a practice of remembering who I've always been—this courageous, calm, connected being. Again and again and again.

Accessing Self

Strengthening Self-Leadership: Evolve It

How might you connect to your Self-energy? This practice invites you to tune into your body, exploring sensations and small adjustments that create comfort and ease. Let this be your moment for self-care and connection.

Settle in

Find a comfortable seated position, whatever feels most natural and comfortable for you—whether in a chair, cross-legged or supported by cushions.

Easy breaths

Close down the eyes and let yourself come into an easy nasal breath. Can you breathe so gently that your inhale and exhale become nearly silent?

Body scan

Check in with your body starting from the top of your head down to the soles of your feet. Let each sensation guide you toward small adjustments that create more comfort.

Self hug

As you continue to breathe, wrap your arms gently around your body in a big warm hug. Say a gentle thank-you for making this time for yourself.

Inspired by: Nahid de Belgeonne

Check In On Your Parts
Strengthening Self-Leadership: Evolve It

Take a few minutes each day to connect with your different internal parts, like checking in with dear friends. Like building any relationship, consistency matters more than duration. Even 5 minutes of genuine attention each day helps your parts feel more seen, soothed, safe, and secure. Begin by:

1. **Connecting to Self:** Place one hand on your heart, the other on your belly. Take a few slow breaths until you feel grounded and calm. Let your Self's natural curiosity and compassion emerge.

2. **Checking in with parts:** When you've connected with your Self-energy, ask your parts these key questions:

    Who's here right now and would like to be heard?
    Notice any emotions, body sensations, or thoughts that arise.

    What are you most concerned about today?
    Listen without trying to fix or change anything.

    What support do you need from me?
    Your parts may want acknowledgment, protection, or comfort.

    What would help you feel safer or more relaxed?
    Sometimes small adjustments can make a big difference.

    Is there anything else you'd like me to know?
    Leave space for whatever else needs to be expressed.

Inspired by: Richard Schwartz

Unburdening Ceremony

*Strengthening Self-Leadership:
Experiment With It*

When parts of us carry burdens from past experiences, they need a safe and sacred way to let them go. Just as we create ceremonies to mark important life transitions, our inner parts benefit from ceremonial release of what they've been carrying. This R.E.L.E.A.S.E tool honors both the weight of what's been carried and the freedom that comes with letting go.

1. **Ready your space:** Find a quiet, comfortable place that feels sacred to you. Light a candle or gather meaningful objects.

2. **Enter within:** Take easy, calm breaths, and turn your attention inward. Which part needs to unburden?

3. **Listen deeply:** What is this part carrying? What does it want you to understand? Notice images, feelings, or memories that arise.

4. **Express gratitude:** Thank your part for how it has protected you all this time.

5. **Ask for permission:** Check if your part is ready to release its burden to earth, air, fire, water, or light.

6. **Set it free:** Perform your release (write what you're releasing on paper and burn it safely; release flowers into moving water; dance in the sunset).

7. **Embrace renewal:** Speak words of welcome to your transformed part (*"I see your strength," "We are free to begin anew"*) and notice what feels different.

Inspired by: Julia Sullivan, Suzan McVicker, Gregg Paisley and Pete Patton

Additional Resources

If you're looking for more practical evidence-based tools to free yourself of your 'good girl' beliefs and embody your unique self, join our community at **www.thegoodgirlgamechangers.com**.

Be sure to:

- Grab our subversive adult storybook, *'The Perfectly Imperfect Little Girl,'* that flips the script on traditional tales.
- Take the free five-minute 'Good Girl' Mindset Survey.
- Enjoy our podcasts and dive deeper into the practices featured with the leading researchers featured throughout the journal.

We'd love to see you there!

Acknowledgements

With our heartfelt thanks...

They say it takes a village to raise a child. We've discovered it takes one to birth a book too. Not just any village—but one filled with women brave enough to lay their stories bare, to show us their scars and their healing, to whisper "me too" when we thought we were alone. Thousands of women opened their lives to our research, each one proving that breaking free from 'good girl' beliefs isn't just possible—it's happening right now, in kitchens and boardrooms and therapy offices across the world.

And then there are the wisdom-keepers, the researchers who've spent decades studying what we felt in our bones—that there's another way to be. Kristin Neff, Carol Dweck, Elise Loehnen, Sue Marriott, Jules Taylor Shore, Tori Olds, and Nahid de Belgeonne didn't just share their findings on our Good Girl Game Changers podcast; they offered us a map through the wilderness, marking the path for anyone brave enough to follow. Our deepest gratitude goes to Ashley Lackovich-Van Gorp, whose PhD research about the mothers of Titira in Ethiopia inspired us to start asking how women around the world are breaking free from society's 'good girl' expectations—even in circumstances that seem impossible.

From Chelle

To my mother: We haven't always walked an easy path, but even in our hardest moments, love has been our compass. The same love that gave you the strength to shatter 'good girl' expectations when it mattered most—fleeing violence, raising children alone, believing in possibilities when the world said there were none. In breaking free, you taught me how to break free too. You were my first glimpse of what being 'uniquely you' could look like as you chose fierce love over fearful compliance. Even now, decades later, I am still learning from the courage of that choice.

Thank you for being brave enough to read these pages. Thank you for being willing to see each other here—not just in the moments of joy and triumph, but in the hard places too, the ones where love and pain got tangled up together. Everything I am today—my strength, my resilience, my compassion—I learned first from watching you.

From Evie

To my parents (the ol' cheezel & mama bear): You were young hippies in love, daring to live life on your own terms. From you, I learned to lead with love, to find beauty in the unconventional, and to embrace a life that feels true to me. Your unwavering support has been my anchor. Even when my choices seemed wild or uncertain, your love and belief in me never wavered. You showed me that the most important thing is to live authentically, with love as my compass.

To my partner (sweet biscuit): Your loyalty, love, and boundless playfulness light up my life in ways I never thought possible. Thank you for making me laugh when I need it most, for standing by me with grace and patience, and for showing me that love can be both solid and joyful. You're my home, my soft place to land.

Also by the Good Girl Game Changers

www.ingramcontent.com/pod-product-compliance
Lightning Source LLC
Chambersburg PA
CBHW042321090526
44585CB00024BA/2785